Ulrike Schamoni

Donald Antrim is the author of three novels and is a regular contributor to *The New Yorker*. He has received fellowships from the National Endowment for the Arts, the John Simon Guggenheim Memorial Foundation, and the Dorothy and Lewis B. Cullman Center for Scholars and Writers at the New York Public Library. He lives in New York City.

One of *The Village Voice*'s 25 Favorite Books of the Year

A *Kansas City Star* Noteworthy Book of the Year

"Donald Antrim turns his razor-sharp gaze to his eccentric, alcoholic mother, Louanne, focusing on her final turbulent years and brilliantly turning moments of pathos and hilarity into a reluctant—and remarkable—love letter to her."

—*Elle*

"A powerful story . . . deeply felt and carefully crafted . . . Evident throughout are Antrim's considerable narrative gifts. He knows the virtues of conciseness and simplicity and brisk dialogue. But he also knows the occasional necessity of complexity. A difficult idea sometimes needs a more capacious conveyance. And so now and then—gently, artfully—he invites us into a sentence that winds its way down an entire page. Long sentences from inferior writers are clumsy congregations of words. But in Antrim's prose they become the silken threads that lead us through the dark labyrinth and out into the light."

—*The Plain Dealer* (Cleveland)

"This memoir is as interesting for its defenses as for its disclosures, and its author's acceptance of the wrenchingly absurd gives it an unlikely charm. . . . Antrim protects his mother even as he unsparingly enumerates her lapses and shortcomings, at once paying tribute and enacting a perfect revenge."

—*The New York Times Book Review*

"A memoir glimmering with hard-won beauty and alive with feeling."

—*Newsday*

"Antrim was haunted by his mother, a predicament he proceeds, lovingly, sorrowfully, to trace to its roots."

—*The Boston Globe*

"Darkly entertaining, but also perhaps enlightening, giving readers insight into familial relationships that are poignant but also uplifting."

—*Library Journal*

"*The Afterlife* is the best kind of memoir: lean, chiseled, emotion filtered through painstakingly created character and situation."

—*The Palm Beach Post*

"Unexpected feelings of real, bone-shaking loss—grief for a mother who will never be 'there' again—are what make the book much more than an excavation of family dysfunction."

—*The New York Observer*

"Astonishing."

—*Vanity Fair*

"Antrim writes like a man defusing a bomb—one false move and he and his family will be destroyed. . . . *The Afterlife* opens a new window into Antrim's genius."

—*The Village Voice*

THE AFTERLIFE

DONALD ANTRIM

PICADOR

FARRAR, STRAUS AND GIROUX

NEW YORK

www.picadorusa.com

Picador® is a U.S. registered trademark and is used by Farrar, Straus and Giroux under license from Pan Books Limited.

For information on Picador Reading Group Guides,
please contact Picador.
Phone: 646-307-5259
Fax: 212-253-9627
E-mail: readinggroupguides@picadorusa.com

Parts of this book originally appeared, in different form, in *The New Yorker*.

Designed by Gretchen Achilles

Library of Congress Cataloging-in-Publication Data
Antrim, Donald.
    The afterlife / Donald Antrim.
        p.   cm.
    ISBN-13: 978-0-312-42635-4
    ISBN-10: 0-312-42635-6
    1. Antrim, Donald—Family.   2. Mothers and sons.   I. Title.

PS3551.N85Z46 2006
813'.54—dc22

2006007954

First published in the United States by Farrar, Straus and Giroux

First Picador Edition: June 2007

for my mother

PART I

My mother, Louanne Antrim, died on a fine Saturday morning in the month of August, in the year 2000. She was lying in new purple sheets on a hospital-style bed rolled up next to the green oxygen tanks set against a wall in what was more or less the living room of her oddly decorated, dark and claustrophobic house, down near the bottom of a drive that wound like a rut past a muddy construction site and backyards bordered with chain-link fence, coming to an end in the parking lot that served the cheerless duck pond at the center of the town in which she had lived the last five years of her life, Black Mountain, North Carolina. The occasion for my mother's move to North Carolina from Florida had been the death of her father, Don Self, from a heart attack, in 1995. Don Self's widow, my mother's mother, Roxanne, was at that time beginning her fall into senility, and was, in any case, unequipped to manage the small estate that my grandfather had left in her name. What I mean to say is that my grandmother, who came of age in the Great Depression and who brought away from that era almost no concept of money beyond the idea that it is not good to give too much of it to one's children, was unlikely to continue her husband's tradition of making large monthly transfers into my mother's bank account. Don Self had kept his daughter afloat for a long while—ever since she'd got sober, thirteen years before, and decided that she was an artist and a visionary, ahead of her time—and now, suddenly, it was incumbent on my mother to seize power of attorney over her mother and take control of the portfolio, a coup she might have accomplished from Miami but was better able to arrange through what in the espionage community is known as closework.

Four years later, Roxanne Self passed away. The funeral was held at the Black Mountain Presbyterian Church in September of 1999. A week after that, my mother—barely days after having got, as I heard her proclaim more than once, *"free* of that woman, now I'm going to go somewhere *I* want to go and live *my* life"—went into the hospital with a lung infection and learned that she, too, would shortly be dead.

She was sixty-five and had coughed and coughed for years and years. There had never been any talking to her about her smoking. The news that she had cancer came as no surprise. It had grown in her bronchi and was inoperable. Radiation was held out as a palliative—it might (and briefly did) shrink the tumor enough to allow air into the congested lung—but my mother was not considered a candidate for chemotherapy. She had, during the course of forty years of, as they say, hard living, progressively and inexorably deteriorated. The story of my mother's lifelong deterioration is, in some respects, the story of her life. The story of my life is bound up in this story, the story of her deterioration. It is the story that is always central to the ways in which I perceive myself and others in the world. It is the story, or at any rate it is my role in the story, that allows me never to lose my mother.

With this in mind—the story of my mother and me, my mother *in* me—I will try to tell another story, the story of my attempt, during the weeks and months following her death, to buy a bed.

I should say to keep a bed. I bought several. The first was a big fat Stearns & Foster queen from Bloomingdale's at Fifty-ninth Street and Lexington Avenue, in New York City. My then girlfriend, R., came along to the store, and together we lay down and compared. Shifman? Sealy? Stearns & Foster? Soft? Firm? Pillow top? I watched R. crawl across a mattress; she bounced up and down with her ass in the air, and I found myself thinking, delusionally, about myself in relation to my mother, who had died the week before, At last, I'm *free* of that woman! Now I'm going to buy a great bed and do some fucking and live *my* life.

Two thousand dollars.

Three thousand dollars would have got me a bigger, fatter Stearns & Foster (and, by extension, a bigger, fatter amount of comfort, leading to more contented sleeping, a finer state of love, and, in general, a happier, more productive life) or a nearly top-of-the-line Shifman. The Shifmans were appealing, thanks to the company's advertisements describing traditional (anachronistic?) manufacturing details such as the eight-way, hand-tied box spring; and to its preference for natural fibers (compressed cotton and wool) over synthetic foams.

"What do you think, hon? Do you like the pillow top?"

"The big one over there?"

"Yes."

"That one's great."

"How long will one of these things last? Did the guy say?"

"Donald, get the bed that feels best. You'll be able to buy other beds later."

"Later? What do you mean, later? Later in life?"

"If you get a bed and you don't like it you can send it back. Look. You have thirty days. People send beds back all the time. That's what department stores are for."

"Right."

"Donald, this is something to be excited about! You're buying a great bed for yourself. You deserve it! We should celebrate."

"Yeah."

"Are you okay?"

"Huh?"

"Do you want to try them one more time?"

Which is what we—and, increasingly, *I*, alone—did. I bought bed no. 1 using my debit card in early September 2000, went home, called the store, and refused to have it delivered, then went back and upgraded, in late September, to another and more expensive bed (the pillow top), and refused to have that one delivered, after which I set out on what amounted, in retrospect, to a kind of quest, or even, one might say, a pilgrimage, to many stores, where I tossed and turned and held repetitive, obsessive conversations with professionals and, whenever possible, patient, accompanying friends, my lay public, about beds. Three months passed, during which time I came to learn more than I ever thought I would about mattresses and about the mattress industry in general—not only about how and where the beds are made but about how they are marketed and sold, and to whom—and, as it happened, I

learned about other things besides actual beds. I am referring to
blankets, pillows, and sheets.

It might be helpful at this point to say that, during this time
that was described and possibly defined by compulsive con-
sumerism, I had a keen sense of myself as a matricide. I felt, in
some substantive yet elusive way, that I had had a hand in
killing my mother. And so the search for a bed became a search
for sanctuary, which is to say that the search for a bed became
the search for a place; and of course by *place* I mean *space*, the
sort of approximate, indeterminate space one might refer to
when one says to another person, "I need some space"; and the
fact that space in this context generally consists of feelings did
not prevent me from imagining that the *space*—considered,
against all reason, as a viable location; namely, my bedroom—
could be filled, pretty much perfectly, by a luxury queen-
size bed draped in gray-and-white-striped, masculine-looking
sheets, with maybe a slightly and appropriately feminine ruffled
bed skirt stretched about the box spring. And I imagined, quite
logically, considering my grief over my mother's passing and
over my participation, not only in the event of her death that
August morning but, as a child and as a man, in the larger narrative of her lifelong self-obliteration through alcoholism and
alcoholism's chief symptom and legacy, rage—I imagined, or
fantasized, that, once cozy and secure in the space filled by the
bed, lying alone or with R. atop pillows stacked high like the
pillows on beds photographed for home-decorating magazines,
I might discover who I would be and how I would carry on
without my mother, a woman who had died in a dreary house,
in an uncomfortable bed.

There was not much that anybody could do. My mother in

the final years of her life had become drastically paranoid. She cultivated or was the victim of episodes in which she conversed with figures from mythology and religion, including the Virgin Mary. Trained as a tailor and costumer, she crafted bizarre, well-made garments that resembled and were meant to be worn as vestments in spiritual ceremonies the purpose of which remained unclear. Everything about these garments—the winglike adornments festooning the back panels, the little baubles and totem objects depending from the sleeves or the lapels, the discordant color palettes displayed in fabric pieces stitched one atop the other like elements in a strange collage— spoke to a symbolism that was deeply private. Worn in public, these robes and gowns were guaranteed to cause unease among people accustomed to functioning in society at large. If my mother wore, to an Asheville concert or museum opening, a dark-purple jacket fastened with clown-size buttons and adorned on the front and sides with crisscrossing strips of Thai silk in tropical pastels, a jacket emblazoned on the back with an enormous white medallion topped with gold cloth gathered and bunched to resemble a floral cake decoration, then finished with more strips of colored silk tied off and hung with drapery tassels descending to varying lengths beneath the hemline, she was not merely acting as a free spirit and doing her thing; she was repudiating the patriarchy and proclaiming herself an artist.

Her power to drive people away was staggering. She behaved spitefully and was divisive in her short-lived relationships with the similarly disenfranchised people who became her friends. Her laughter was abrasive, sometimes even frightening. She chewed with her mouth open, often spilling food down her front. Her hair looked at times as if she had cut it herself, in the dark. You were either with her or against her. She believed that her father was not her real father; that her mother had tried to drown her in a pond when she was a child; that her pulmonary specialist wanted to have sex with her; that in death she would be met by Carl Jung, the Virgin Mary, and Merlin the Magician; that she had done her work on earth and that her work was good; that she was one of those who had been chosen to herald the coming new order of beautiful humanity; that in a former life she had died a watery death as a Roman galley slave, shackled to the oars; that men were shits and her children were hostile; that her smoking was her business, so mind your own fucking business; that her son was an artist just like she was; that she and I should go into therapy together.

She was, for anyone close to her, and especially for those depending on her competency, a threatening person. She had, in fact, lived much of her adult life in a blackout, dreamlessly "sleeping" three hours or less most nights. The loss of REM sleep must have had devastating consequences on her body and mind. She went on screaming campaigns that lasted into the wee hours. A few times, I remember, I found her lying on the floor in the living room, early in the morning before dawn.

Perhaps her mother *had* tried to drown her in a pond. The truth may have been as bad as that, or worse. My mother may have been a victim of Munchausen syndrome by proxy, a perversion of caretaking in which a child is subjected to unwarranted medical interventions, even surgeries. It was suspected by her physicians in North Carolina, as well as by members of our family, that my mother's mother had had a curious habit of taking her only child to the doctor. This is not something I can comment on extensively; I wasn't there. And yet I can imagine

9

my grandmother Roxanne, in the late 1940s or thereabouts, leading my mother by the hand down some country hospital's white aisles, or sitting with her in the waiting room in a Florida doctor's office. I remember that my mother told stories, when I was young, of operations. What exactly these operations were meant to achieve is a bit of a mystery. One, it seems to me, had to do with the removal of a rib. And there was a famous story that had my mother "waking up" as her doctors pronounced her dead on the table. By the time I was born, Roxanne had become a radical nutritionist, intent on controlling her family's diets and moods; she handed out vitamins and advice to cancer patients who learned about her on the Florida cancer grapevine; she prescribed foods whose effectiveness in some cases (broccoli, kale) was later confirmed by the national health industry. I believe she saw herself as a folk heroine. It is possible to imagine my mother's death trip as an internalized, masochistically directed act of hatred against her own mother, who used health to suppress everyone around her; and against her father, who, in any number of conceivable scenarios, had been unable to acknowledge how things were for his daughter, or to act as her advocate, in her childhood.

When young, my mother had been popular and a beauty. She was a girl in Tennessee and a teenager in Sarasota, Florida, where she met my father. Together, my parents were, as far as I can tell from their yearbooks, one of those successful, envied high school couples. A friend of theirs, a man who was in love with my mother in college and had never fallen out of love, once described her to me in terms that revealed the force of her sexuality and personality in those days. Because she had no siblings, I have no maternal aunts or uncles who can accurately remember her as a girl. And testimony from my parents' old crowd about later years—after she'd left home, married my father, had her children, and settled down as a wife and mother in graduate school housing—is hard to come by, as are memories of my own, memories of the sort that add up to form a coherent . . . what? Picture? Impression? Narrative? I was four, five, six years old. My sister, Terry, was three, four, five. It was the early sixties, the last years—as I think of that era now, almost forty years after our father fell in love with another woman, and our family began coming apart—of southern intellectualism in the style of the Agrarians, when the newly married Episcopalian children of Presbyterians were reading *Finnegans Wake*, escaping into Ph.D. programs, drinking bourbon, martinis, and bargain beer, and staying up all night quarreling and having affairs and finding out about the affairs, then tossing *their* children into the backseats of VW bugs and driving by night up or down the coast. To this day, I remain unable to reliably document the progress of my parents' migrations and relocations, the betrayals and reconciliations, the reunions, separations, re-relocations, hospitalizations. Suffice it to say that there is no end to the crazy stories, many of which I have already used too many times as opening gambits on dates.

But what about the bed? In December, I allowed delivery of the pillow top. The Bloomingdale's deliverymen carried it up the stairs, and I dressed it with the sheets and pillows that I had collected for this occasion. The bed, in comparison with the futon I had been sleeping on, seemed gigantic. It *was* gigantic; not only broad but tall, it overpowered the bedroom. Its phallic implications were evident in my invitations to R. to "come over and see it." Things should have ended there, with some promising rambunctiousness with R. and a gradual acceptance of a new order in my house. But that would have required me to be a different person and much farther removed in time from my mother's death. It would've required, as well, that I had never heard anything about Dux.

Dux is one of those companies that produce esoteric, expensive products scientifically engineered to transform your life. When you buy a Dux bed, you gain membership in a community of people who have bought and believe in Dux beds. A Dux bed at first seems peculiarly soft; if you stay on one for a while, you may experience yourself as "relaxed" in a way that can actually be alarming. The initial impression is of settling onto a well-calibrated water bed—on a Dux, you really climb *into* bed. The company promises a variety of health benefits, some postural, some having to do with increased deep sleep, all having to do with natural latex and with the myriad coils described in the Dux literature as a "system" that allows the bed to shape itself gently to the body, reducing pressure points and therefore the number of times a sleeping person will shift or move about to get comfortable during the night. "Do you have a Dux?" I have heard the cognoscenti say. Dux beds come with a twenty-year warranty—I seem to remember "The Last Bed You'll Ever Buy" as one of the promotional slogans. The beds are manufactured in Sweden, advertised on classical-music radio stations, sold in company-owned stores that look like spas, and never, ever go on sale.

I don't know how many times, during the early winter of the year my mother died, I marched—typically by myself, though whenever possible with R. or one of those other aforementioned friends—into the Duxiana store on East Fifty-eighth Street (conveniently adjacent to Bloomingdale's), where I pulled off my shoes and hopped from bed to bed and read and reread the brochures and harassed Pamela, the manager, with every kind of question about this model versus that. I arranged the goose-down pillows. I settled in. I turned onto my side. I turned onto my other side. Wonderful. You could choose mahogany or metallic legs that would elevate the bed to a great height, or you could leave the bed low to the floor, in the manner of beds in sleek European hotels. You could tuck the sheets in this way, drape them that way. Cotton top pad? Or latex? I began to sense, during afternoons reclining at the Dux store, that all the decisions I might make from here on out could flow naturally from the purchase of the right bed. Though I already had my new (returnable) bed in my bedroom, I didn't especially like it. I lacked sufficient *desire* to like the bed. It is true that the bed was large, but in every other respect I found it pedestrian and a letdown, because it was not saving my relationship with R. It was not making my apartment feel like home. It was not writing my book. Worst of all—and this was the failing that hurt the most—it was not allowing me to carry on indefinitely in my search for a bed.

How badly did I want a Dux? I wanted one in exactly the manner and proportion that was appropriate with regard to the product.

I wanted one enough to want to buy one.

It was in this way that a novelist with literary-level sales and a talent for remorse came to lay out close to seven thousand dollars for a mattress.

—Almost.

In the year preceding my mother's death, a year that was

characterized by the kind of mood oscillations that accompany the routine progress toward failure of medical therapeutic interventions in advanced cancer cases—the tidal-seeming, almost manic rising and falling, with every piece of news, every stressed-out conversation with Mom or her doctors, of hope and depression, hope and depression, hope and renewed hope and more hope, followed by distracted euphoria and a deeper despair and the weird, impulsive anger that can be directed at practically anybody at any time, the continuum of fear and volatility that is familiar in some form or another to just about anyone who has watched a parent or a child, or a husband or a wife or a lover or a friend, get a little better, then a little worse, then a little better, dying according to the program, as it were—during this year, I more or less stopped working, and I stopped exercising. I read less, went out for dinner with friends less, made love less. I am a cyclist, and for years have had a routine of riding training laps around the park near where I live. My body has been accustomed to this regimen in which a great amount of physical information is available to me, information in the form of sensations that come with deep inhalations and exhalations as I walk down the street or, while riding, stand in the pedals to climb a hill; or in the awareness I might have of a gain or a loss in my weight; or in the excitement I can feel when touching another person, or when being touched; information in the form of, I suppose, *myself*, proprioceptively living in space. Little by little, that information disappeared. In the dull absence of myself, I did what my mother had done throughout her life. I sat up nights in my kitchen, smoking.

People are fond of saying that the truth will make you free. But what happens when the truth is not one simple, brutal thing? I could not imagine life without my mother. And it was true as well that only without her would I feel able to live. I had had enough of Louanne Antrim and was ready for her to be gone. I wanted her dead, and I knew that, in the year of her dying, I would neglect her.

I would and I did. In this, at least, I can claim I was faithful to her—to *us*. I was, after all, her man. It had been my impossible and defining task to be both like and unlike all other men—more specifically, like and unlike her father and her errant, excommunicated ex-husband, my father. What does this mean? I'm not sure I can clearly say. I was, I suppose, never to leave her for another woman. I was never to lie to or deceive her. When I first began to write and publish novels, it was understood by my mother, and hence unwittingly by me, that I was exhibiting, in whatever could be called my artistic accomplishments, *her* creative agency, her gifts.

"I'll come down soon and stay a few days, Mom."

"You don't have to come."

"I want to come."

"I'm not expecting you."

"I'll come."

"Don't if you don't want to."

"Mom."

"Don't wait too long. I'm going to die soon."

"How do you know?"

"Dr. McCarrick is trying to kill me."

"Excuse me?"

"He won't take my calls."

"He's a doctor."

"What's that supposed to mean?"

"Nothing. It's a joke. Sort of. He's busy. Doctors are busy. Never mind."

"Everyone is against me. You're against me."

"Mom, he's not trying to kill you. No one is trying to kill you. No one wants to kill you."

I put off the visit. I put it off. A dog in the apartment next to mine started barking, and for a while I lost my mind. Then the dog stopped barking and a year had passed and my sister and I were boarding flights from opposite ends of the country to stand beside my mother's bed in the little house near the bottom of the hill that pitched down to the parking lot beside the town lake. It was our practice, my sister's and mine, to fly into Charlotte, rendezvous at the airport car-rental desk, get the car, stop off at Bridges, in Shelby, North Carolina, for barbecue, then head west over the mountains, past Chimney Rock, up around Old Fort, and down into Black Mountain. The drive took three hours. We could have flown to Asheville, thirty minutes from our mother's house, but Terry and I traveled this roundabout way, I think, in order to give ourselves time to prepare for the ordeal of being—for one last time, in this case—Louanne's children in Louanne's house. That day, we managed to be in a hurry and to drive slowly at the same time. Terry talked about her children and about a neighbor who, like our mother, had refused nutrition in the final stages of a terminal illness. It was late on a late-summer afternoon. The farms and weathered churches alongside the two-lane highway had never seemed to me so lonely or so lovely, so beckoning, as they did that afternoon. This was our grandfather's country; and it was his father's, and his father's father's; and it was our mother's and, for that brief time—looking out the car windows at the sights along the way, at touristy Lake Lure and the rocky stream descending the grade in low waterfalls beside the road; at the forlorn houses surrounded by irregularly shaped fields planted with corn and beans; at the kudzu that devours more and more of the South, forest and field, every year—it was ours, too. I remember thinking that, after she died, there would be no one left to bind me to this part of the world, and I wondered what might lead me, in the future, ever to return.

At the house, we found our mother on the hospital bed in the living room. Beside the bed stood the enormous wooden table on which she had measured and scissored fabrics. Bolts of silk leaned in a corner. Bookshelves held paperbacks about Carl Jung and healing. The day nurse left Terry and me alone. Our mother was on her way to dying. She had informed us, earlier in the summer, that sometime before too long, probably before her birthday in September, she would, as she had put it, "take matters into my own hands," but she had not told us exactly when; there were celestial and astrological considerations that needed factoring, and she was waiting for the right moment. Now the moment had come. Gazing at her emaciated face in the evening light, I discovered something that Terry had known and I hadn't, which was that our mother used dentures. These had been taken out. Her mouth was collapsed. She made noises and sounds that could not be interpreted as sentences, or even words. Morphine, dropped off earlier by the Hospice workers, waited, sealed, in a bottle in the kitchen. No one, not even the nurse, seemed to know precisely when to begin feeding it to her. So, like the morphine in the bottle in the kitchen, we waited, and the next day my mother "woke"—as the dying sometimes will, briefly—and spoke relatively straightforwardly, if disjointedly, about her past. She called up names of people from Charlottesville and Kingsport and Miami, from Knoxville and Gainesville, Johnson City and Sarasota and Tallahassee. We felt her feet; her feet were warm. My sister gave her a sponge bath and changed her clothes, and we arranged the pillows beneath her head, and the nurse put her teeth in, and my mother asked us, in her broken voice, if we would mind, please, bringing her a martini.

Playing the role of guardian, playing at being powerful, I asked if she thought a martini a good idea, and she answered, quite sensibly, "What harm could it do now?"

Had there been gin and vermouth in the house, I would surely have mixed her a cocktail. Or maybe I wouldn't have. Did I offer her a taste of beer? I don't remember. Was she still taking oxygen? I can't remember that, either. Green tanks and plastic hoses were everywhere. The part-time nurse practitioner, a sweet and competent, though hardly medically knowledgeable, hard-line Christian fundamentalist, and my mother's two female friends, pagan Wiccans as far as I could make out, were in a battle over my mother's soul. It was a minor flare-up of social conflicts in the New South of the old Appalachias— the Christers versus the Shamans—staged over the proxy that was Louanne Antrim's wasted body. Back and forth it went, in whispered private conferences, little peace talks out in the yard:

"They're saying occult things. They're going to hand her over to the Devil. I've got three churches praying for your mom to rise into Jesus' arms."

"That Pentecostal girl's trying to convert Louanne to

Christ. Your mother left organized religion behind a long time ago. It's not what she wants."

"Every time I pray for your mom, they come in and they stop me. I'm just worried sick over your mom."

In the end, it fell to me to administer the morphine. I should say that I decided, as the man on the scene, to be the one to give the morphine. Every four hours, I pressed a lorazepam tablet to powder in a spoon, introduced into this powder a small measure of the liquid morphine, drew the solution into an oral syringe, and squirted the drug into my mother's partly open mouth. I was careful to squirt toward the side of her mouth. My sister and I swabbed her dry lips with sponges. On the third night her death rattle began. I put on Mozart piano sonatas, but after a while, getting into the spirit of things, I switched to Miles Davis. At some point before dawn, my mother's face relaxed and her skin cleared, and, though her throat and chest still rattled terribly, she smiled. It was a broad, unambiguous smile. Terry said to me, "Look, she's getting younger." It was true. In the hours before she died, Louanne began to resemble herself as the young woman we had seen in photographs taken before we were born—full of radiance and with her future and whatever crazed or credible hopes she had ahead of her. Amazingly, this effect occurred in spite of the absence of teeth. I sat in a chair beside the bed and read to her from *The Collected Stories of Peter Taylor*, which she did not seem to appreciate at all—her smile vanished and she actually scowled at the opening to "A Wife of Nashville"—and, though I like Peter Taylor well enough, I felt in that instant real camaraderie with my mother. I left off reading and told her that she had been a good mother, a good artist; that Terry and I loved her and were grateful to her for her care; that those years in Tallahassee, in particular, had been pretty good years; that both of us, both her children, however much we might miss her, had a great deal to live for; that we would be all right without her. The sun came up. Terry drove back to the hotel for a shower and a nap. The New Agers and the kind Christian were away somewhere; and I held my mother's hand and told her that the house was empty except for the two of us, it was just her and me in the house, and it was a nice day outside the windows, birds were in the trees, a breeze blew the leaves, clouds crossed the sky, and if she wanted to she could go ahead and die, which she promptly did.

From 1966 until the summer of 1968, my sister and I lived with our mother in Tallahassee, Florida. Across the street from us was a church whose steeple had been removed and laid on its side to peel and rust in the yard beside the church. At the top of the street was a gas station where Apalachicola oysters could be bought for five dollars a bushel. Our father was teaching in Virginia; though our parents' first divorce was either final or on the way to being so, he visited monthly, pulling up in his black Volkswagen Beetle, parking in the driveway made of seashells and sand—the cue for Terry and me to rush from the house screaming with excitement. Often, the first evening of his visit we would spend as a family, sitting on the concrete-and-brick porch, shucking and eating dozens of oysters and looking out at the church with its decapitated, useless steeple. My sister and I conspire to remember these as good years, primarily because there was sparingly little head-to-head conflict between our parents, given that they were infrequently together; but also because the three of us, Terry, my mother, and I, became a family of our own, a family that existed in the absence of the family we wished we could be. Terry and I did fine in school; we rode our bikes, built forts using lawn furniture, played with friends from across the street. I joined the Cub Scouts; she was a Brownie. Occasionally, our mother allowed us to stay home from school, and our party of three became a tea party in the living room. There was something approaching normalcy in our lives. In retrospect, I would say that it was a forced normalcy. Our happy family was a worrisomely happy performance of family.

This calls to mind a particular event. When I was nine, I got to play the part of Young Macduff in a Florida State University production of *Macbeth*. My mother worked as an assistant costumer in the theater department. It was she who would eventually make my costume, a yellow-orange tunic with a sash for a belt. The tunic, despite repeated washing, became bloodier and bloodier with each performance. Here are some lines from act IV, scene 2, spoken by Lady Macduff and her son, before they are murdered by Macbeth's henchmen:

L. MACD.: Sirrah, your father's dead,
            And what will you do now? How will you live?
SON: As birds do, mother.
L. MACD.: What, with worms and flies?
SON: With what I get, I mean; and so do they.
L. MACD.: Poor bird! thou'dst never fear the net nor lime,
            The pitfall nor the gin.
SON: Why should I, mother? Poor birds they are not set for.
    My father is not dead, for all your saying.

L. MACD.: Yes, he is dead. How wilt thou do for a father?

SON: Nay, how will you do for a husband?

And:

SON: Was my father a traitor, mother?

L. MACD.: Ay, that he was.

SON: What is a traitor?

L. MACD.: Why, one that swears and lies.

SON: And be all traitors that do so?

L. MACD.: Every one that does so is a traitor, and must be hang'd.

It is but a moment before the killers enter. The stage directions call for Young Macduff to be murdered first, crying out, "He has kill'd me, mother: Run away, I pray you!" and for her to flee into the wings, crying "Murther!" In our production, both deaths occurred onstage. First I went down, stabbed in the back and in the stomach. My pretend mother ran to my side and knelt beside me. Then she was killed. She fell across me and lay dead (though breathing heavily). It was in this way that I came to fall in love with Lady Macduff. I mean that I fell in love with Janice, the college girl playing Lady Macduff. The lights dimmed to end the scene. Each night, I watched from beneath my mother who was not my mother, as the lights' filaments faded; and, when the stage fell dark, I whispered in Janice's ear, which was practically in my mouth, "Okay, get up," because the smell of her, and her hair falling across my face, and her ear in my mouth, and the pressure and heat of her body pressing down on mine became too intense to bear.

It seems to me that some of the archetypes for my adult life were introduced during the period of the play: the man who appears and withdraws, appears and withdraws; the woman who is both my mother and a girl on whom I have a crush; and the real mother, who dies for want of the love and protection of a man, her husband. These are rudimentary formulations; nevertheless, they point to a fact of large consequence, the fact of my precarious victory over my father and my attainment of my mother. Like Young Macduff in the moments before death, I became my mother's confidant. In doing so, I became her true husband, the man both like and unlike other men. And, in becoming these things, I became sick.

My main ailment was a debilitating asthma that required trips to hospitals and doctors' offices. I swallowed drugs that kept me awake nights, struggling to breathe mist from an atomizer that hummed away on the table next to my bed, while my mother sat at my side. She had a way of sitting beside me on the bed—at a certain angle, leaning over, maybe touching my forehead or holding my hand, perched the way mothers everywhere perch on beds beside sick children—that I will never forget. This was our intimacy. In later years, after she and my father had remarried, and her alcoholic deterioration had begun in earnest, the image of her in the Tallahassee days, serving tea in china cups, or sitting up nights with me on the edge of my bed in the little house on Eighth Street, would be supplanted by the more violent image of the increasingly damaged Lady Macbeth she was to become. When we say about something or someone that we are dying for that thing, that person, we may miss the more literal meaning hidden in the metaphor. I was a boy dying *for* his mother, angrily, stubbornly doing her work of dying, the work she had begun before I was born. In this version of the story of my illness—the story of our collusion in illness—I was not merely bringing my mother to my bedside, not simply bringing her close. Rather, I was marrying myself to her, learning to speak the language of her unconscious, which, as time would bear out, was a language of suffocation and death. In sickness, we were joined: she was I and I was she.

I bought the Dux. Of course I bought top of the line. If you're going to buy a brand-new rest of your life, why go halfway? The guys who brought it in and set it up were not only deliverymen; they were true believers, real aficionados. One of the men was large, the other less large. The large man did the talking.

"This is the bed I sleep on."

"Really?"

"Best bed I ever slept on. I've slept on every kind of bed. Take a look at me. I'm a big guy. Most beds, I'd get two, three years and the things wear out. Not this bed."

"Really?"

"I'm telling you. I sleep on this bed. My mother sleeps on this bed. My sister has one of these beds. My mother's sister sleeps on this bed."

"You're kidding."

"Sleep like a baby."

Like a baby? What if I wanted to sleep like a man? It didn't much matter either way, because I wasn't going to get any sleep at all. Not that night. Not the following night. Not the night after that.

"Hey, come over. I got the bed."

"You did?"

"Yeah. It's here."

"I can't believe you got the bed."

"I got the bed. It's here."

"Have you gotten on it?"

"Kind of."

"Have you put the sheets on it?"

"Uh-huh."

"Is my pillow on it?"

"Of course."

"Is it as tall as the other bed?"

"Just about."

"You got the bed!"

"I got the bed!"

Talk about up all night—however, not for reasons one would anticipate or wish. It was a bad night on many counts. In the first place, the bed felt too soft. In the second place, it was too springy. In the third place, it seemed too transmissive of vibrations caused by movement. In the fourth place, it was too final. It represented the end of the quest for itself. And now, here it was. The bed was mine. It would be the place not of love and rest but of deprivation and loneliness. All during that first night, I lay awake and *felt* the bed. I felt myself sinking into it. I felt, sinking into the bed, the absence of familiar pressures against my shoulders and hips; and, without those familiar pressures, I felt adrift. If R. moved even an inch, I felt that. If she turned over, the effect was catastrophic. In the morning I was wrung out, and so was R.

What followed over the next few days was a workshop in hysteria. I called the store. I phoned other stores, in other states. I wanted to know from the Dux community what I could do to join in, to make myself on my bed feel the way they said they felt on theirs. Pamela, the manager of the store on East Fifty-eighth Street, lost patience eventually and told me that she would take the bed back—immediately! Against company policy! She'd make an exception in my case! Though not for a full refund! Did I want the bed? Did I want the bed or not? Alone at night, I sank into the bed and tried to want it. And the farther I sank into it the closer I came to knowing what the bed was. It was the last bed I would ever buy. It was the bed that would deliver me into my fate. It was the bed that would marry me again to my mother, the bed Louanne and I would share. When I moved, the bed moved, talking back to me through the echoing of coiled springs, telling me that there would be no rest for me. The bed was alive. It was alive with my mother. I sank into the bed, and it was as if I were sinking down into her arms. She was not beside me on the bed, she was *inside* the bed, and I was *inside* the bed; and she was pulling me down into the bed to die with her. It was my deathbed. It was a coffin. It was a sarcophagus. I didn't want to die. Did I? If only I could get the bed to stay still. Why wouldn't the bed leave me alone? Why wouldn't the bed be *my* bed?

In the daytime I worked the phones. A woman in a southern state referred me to a man in the same southern state who had sold these beds for twenty years. This man knew everything about the beds.

"What kind of floor is your bed on? Is it a wood floor?"

"Yes, it is a wood floor."

"There's your problem."

"How do you mean?"

"Sometimes on a wood floor these beds can be very reverberant. Do you have carpet under the bed?"

"No."

"You need carpet under the bed. That'll damp the springs."

"I don't have any carpet."

"Go out and get yourself a set of those felt-and-rubber furniture coasters. You'll need six, because on a queen-size bed there are those extra legs supporting the middle of the bed."

Coasters? It was too late for coasters. The bed had to go back to the warehouse! It had to go back the next morning! The large man and the less large man were coming to haul away the bed that I both wanted and did not want, that I both needed and did not need in order to continue being a man who was both better and worse than other men. I ran out, minutes before the stores closed, bought the coasters, ran back home, and shoved them under the legs of the bed. I bounced on the bed. I hadn't slept in days. Nights. And on and on the night went: My mother. The bed. My mother. The bed. Morphine. The bed. I'd failed her by living. I'd killed her with negligence. Comfort was forbidden. Except in death. In the morning, the men were coming to cart away our bed. I pulled up the covers and sank into the bed and drifted restlessly in that half-awake dream world where I could live and die with and without my dead mother, and I waited for the men.

Then it was morning and the light through the windows was hurting my eyes and I had a cigarette of my own going, and the buzzer rang and they tromped up the stairs and began packing the bed. They took off the legs and broke it down and wrapped it up, and just like that the bedroom was empty, and my mind without sleep was suddenly empty, too.

"Wait!"

They waited.

"This isn't right!"

"What's not right?"

"Everything! All of it!"

I told them the story of the bouncy, springy bed. All that sleeplessness. All those phone calls. The store managers, the furniture coasters. It all poured out. Not about my mother, though. Nothing about Louanne. The men stood in my empty bedroom, listening, paying attention. The large man, who had, I think, a firm grasp of reality, said, "I see that there is a problem. But I have to tell you, I'm just the driver."

I went to the telephone. I called the number for the Swedish president of Dux Interiors in North America. What in the world was I going to say to him? What did I want from him?

"Hello?"

"Hello. Is this Mr. Gustafsson?"

"Speaking."

"Hi. My name is Donald. I'm a customer? I have a bed that's being picked up and returned."

"Returned?"

"Yeah, well."

"You don't like the bed?"

"I like the bed. I like the bed. It's just that there are problems."

"Problems?"

The large man stepped forward. He took control. He said to me, "Let me talk to Bo."

I gave the large man the phone. He stood in my ravaged,

empty bedroom and did the talking. He talked for a long time. When he was finished speaking with the president, he passed me my phone. He told me, "Bo wants to talk to you."

"Hello?"

"Hello. Is it Donald? Hello. Let me ask you something. What size bed do you have?"

"Queen."

"Ah. And you say it is too bouncy?"

"That's part of it."

"Hmm."

"It's reverberant."

"Reverberant? Explain."

"I mean you can feel everything. When you're on the bed. When you're in bed. You feel too much. I feel too much."

"Well. I don't know what to tell you. There are many springs in that bed. That is how it works. All the springs work together. There is going to be some movement. Maybe to get a good night's rest you need your own sleeping area. Maybe you need the king."

"I don't have room for a king."

"I don't know what to tell you. You have to decide if you want to keep the bed or not. I cannot decide for you."

"I know."

"The bed is a good bed. I am sure that if you keep it you will get used to it. These beds take some getting used to."

"I know."

"Good luck."

I hung up the phone. I saw the men standing in my house. I saw the crated bed by the door. I saw the sunlight coming through the windows. I saw myself standing there seeing these things. I was a man whose need for love and sympathy had led him to telephone a Swedish executive in the middle of the morning. Perhaps, at some point, the story of my mother and the bed becomes the story of my mother and father, the story that remains to be told, the story, you could say, of the queen versus the king.

The bed went away. I let it go. R. was right. I could get another bed later. I stood in my empty room. In place of the bed was—shame? In place of the bed was a question, a question that is at once too simple and too complicated to answer.

PART II

or a time when I was a boy, my father's brother, my uncle Eldridge—a man, as I think of him now, both like and unlike other men—became my friend and companion. Today I cannot think of my uncle without remembering his car and the things he carried in it. In the backseat he kept a bicycle with the front wheel removed. I never saw him put the wheel on and ride. Next to the bicycle was a golf bag holding woods and irons, balls, tees, pencils for scoring, golf gloves, a visor. Adjacent to the clubs were a couple of beach chairs folded and jammed between the car's front and backseats, and wedged on the seat were towels and a cooler chest, into which he loaded, every day or two, ice, beer, and strawberry, grape, and orange sodas. In the car's trunk, as I remember it, were his tennis racquets with their protective covers zippered on, and a tennis bag like those the pros carry onto the court, stuffed with balls in cans, cotton sweatbands, shorts, shirts, tennis shoes, socks, and a hat. There was a football for playing catch at the beach, and a pump for pumping up the ball. There were baseball mitts and a baseball; and there was fishing gear—a takedown rod stored in its elegant cylindrical case, and a small tackle kit packed with hooks, lures, and line—and there was swimming and, sometimes, I recall, scuba equipment, including a mask, fins, a snorkel, a dive knife, a depth gauge, a regulator, a buoyancy vest, a weight belt, and, shoved up into the back of the trunk—though in order to make space for it, he might have been forced, in a gesture of triage, to sacrifice other items—a small tank that actually belonged to me. In the event that he had occasion to dress nicely on land, he had what was minimally required. Pressed trousers. A clean shirt. A tie, rolled up. Changes of underwear. Thin socks. A belt. Black shoes with shoe trees inserted in them. Shoe polish. A rag for polishing. There was a shaving kit holding a razor and soap, shampoo, talcum powder, a toothbrush and toothpaste, a hairbrush and a comb, and plenty of the English Leather cologne he splashed on at intervals throughout his day. There was a battery-operated portable record player, and Everly Brothers, Clancy Brothers, and Smothers Brothers records to play on it. For reading, he carried a collection of hunting, tennis, golf, and archery magazines, *Playboy* and *Penthouse*, and books by D. H. Lawrence, Henry Miller, and Lawrence Durrell. For shooting, he kept, in a space near the tire well, a .22 pistol in a leather case; and sometimes there was a double-barreled shotgun; and, when he had the shotgun packed in the car and planned to do some shooting with it, there might also be a cardboard box containing clay pigeons, many of which I threw for him, using a spring-loaded contraption designed for manually launching the fragile yellow disks. There was no shortage of ammo. And there were many things relating to the maintenance of the car in specific and to safe travel in general: spark plugs, antifreeze in a jug, motor oil in a can, socket wrenches, jumper cables, sulfur flares. There was tanning lotion; and there were Band-Aids and other medical supplies, including an Ace bandage; and writing materials and postage stamps; and, tucked here and there in nooks and crannies, golf shoes, an umbrella, a rain poncho, a thermos, a Swiss Army knife, bottle and can openers, a pair of binoculars, a Frisbee.

On days off from his job, loading Canada Dry delivery trucks at a warehouse near the airport in Sarasota, Florida, he used to golf or lie on the beach or play tennis at the municipal courts with his friends from work, and sometimes he'd drive to a secluded place in the woods, where he would set up one of the folding beach chairs, place beside it the cooler and a handful of his books and magazines, put a record on the record player, and sit listening to folk music, flipping through the magazines, looking at the world through his binoculars, sipping beer, and, every now and then, shooting pistol rounds at empty cans he'd propped on tree branches or rotting fence posts in the distance. One day, according to my mother, state and federal agents surrounded him, then handcuffed him and took him into custody, because he had been spotted by surveillance teams sent in advance of President Nixon, who was about to land in Sarasota on *Air Force One*. When the agents took him to the local police station, the chief of police told them, "Oh, that's just Bob Antrim, he doesn't mean a bit of harm," which was true enough; and so they promptly let him go.

His name was Robert Eldridge Antrim. He was known in his family as Eldridge to distinguish him from his father, also Robert, and among his friends as Bob, but he was also occasionally called Sam. The name Sam in relation to my uncle first appeared in the mid-fifties, in the sports pages of a Sarasota newspaper, in an article glorifying the Sarasota High School golf team, for which Eldridge was a star player. In fact, it was

Eldridge who had reported his name as Sam, presumably because he had grown tired of Eldridge. It was a joke; and the joke stuck, though by the end of his life the only person still calling him Sam was my mother, who was with him at the Sarasota Memorial Hospital when he died, in 1992, of acute alcohol poisoning. When I was young, I knew my uncle as Eldridge. For a few years, when I was a teenager, he was a hero to me. Today, when I think of him, he is Bob, and I think this transformation from Eldridge to Bob by way of Sam has something to do with the effect he had on my life, in particular the effect of a single incident that took place when I was fourteen years old.

We were living in Miami, my mother, my father, my sister, our absurd cats—Zelda Fitzgerald and the neurologically impaired Siamese, Justine—and I. Eldridge, during those years, the early seventies, lived up the Gulf Coast in Sarasota, in a suburban tract house he shared with his mother, my grandmother Eliza. The story of Eliza's life is, in some ways, unusual for a woman of her time. She grew up during the early years of the twentieth century, in Richmond, Virginia, in what was, according to my father, a strict Episcopalian home ruled by a patriarch who was stern with his sons and possessively doting toward his only daughter, who nevertheless managed to escape to nearby Randolph-Macon Woman's College, and then to Columbia University, where she earned a master's degree in Spanish. During her years away at school, a medical student from San Juan, Puerto Rico, took up residence—I don't know the particulars of the arrangement—in her father's house. Over the course of her vacations at home, Eliza fell in love with this man, and even went so far as to board ship and sail with him to

Puerto Rico to visit his home. Rafael was, according to family lore, the love of my grandmother's life. I imagine him as a person formed in a certain European mold: erudite and very likely soft-spoken, a man wearing clothes made to draw attention away from his physique, from, as it were, his person—not in order to obscure the fact that he is, in my mental picture of him, neither tall nor fit but, rather, to hide, out of sheer politeness, his intrinsic attractiveness, which is to say his unsuitability as a life partner for a young woman brought up in an essentially Victorian household. About matters so far removed in time and sensibility from one's own, one can only guess. My father told me that when Rafael's stay in America ended he begged Eliza to marry him. She made it clear that she loved him but could never marry a Catholic. And that, apparently, was that. Her lover went home without her. They saw each other once or twice again over the years. And then, when she was very old and in failing health, as if bearing out the eroticism inherent in loving a person one cannot bring oneself to marry, she did something surprising and beautiful. She bought a plane ticket for San Juan. She did not tell anyone her intentions. She appears to have had no specific intentions. Alone in Puerto Rico, she visited the places she remembered from her time there with Rafael, who had died a year or two earlier.

Eliza's life, it seems to me, turned out quite differently from whatever she might have hoped for when she was a woman in her twenties, taking flight, however incompletely or abortively, from her father's house. It is my understanding that after she returned home from New York she lived for a time in a sort of domestic captivity, like a Virginian Elizabeth Barrett Browning, until it was arranged that she would marry a distant cousin,

Robert Antrim, a man older than she, a man she likely did not love passionately. Robert Antrim was in those years the manager of the Blandy Experimental Farm, now the Virginia State Arboretum, a University of Virginia teaching farm near Winchester. He was taciturn and hardworking, and he and Eliza had two sons. Then one day Robert Antrim took it into his head that it was his destiny to raise gladioli in Florida. He and his brother, Frank, had for some time been going on annual car trips together—speechless two-week-long excursions to central Florida and back. They had an old Ford, and were known for driving slowly.

I can remember, from my childhood, my father's father's slow driving. Many years after Robert and his brother took their first trips down the Atlantic seaboard, and long after Robert Antrim had settled his family in Sarasota, near the end of his life, when my sister and I were young, he used to drive us, in his blue Mercedes diesel sedan, to the Ringling Museum of the Circus, part of the grandiose folly of an estate left by the great John Ringling after he fell into debt and, in 1936, the same year my father was born, died of pneumonia. The Ringling complex is located on Sarasota Bay, and includes John and Mable Ringling's enormous and weirdly decorated winter residence, Cà d'Zan; and the Ringling Art Museum filled with minor Old Masters and Baroque paintings and tapestries; and a theater in the Italian Baroque style, the Asolo; and the Museum of the Circus, all originally constructed using buildings and parts of buildings painstakingly disassembled, crated up, and shipped from northern Italy to Florida in the 1920s and early thirties. Attached to the painting galleries is a library in which my father, in his free time as a young museum guide working afternoons after school and over summer vacations, read art history. It was here, according to my mother, that Sir Anthony Blunt, the infamous spy and historian of Renaissance and Baroque art, upon finishing a tour of the museum's collections, invited my father, who had conducted the tour, to attend the Courtauld Institute in London. This took place before Blunt was exposed as a Russian agent and stripped of his knighthood. I sometimes wonder how things might have gone in our family had my father accepted Sir Anthony's offer. In the event, things were as they were, which meant that my sister and I, when children in Sarasota, were unfailingly greeted, at the entrance to the Museum of the Circus, by Cookie, a midget wearing an ornate red coat. Cookie was famous as the Munchkin who, in the Munchkinland sequence in *The Wizard of Oz*, presents Dorothy with a bouquet.

Anyway, I remember from those trips that my grandfather never drove his Mercedes at a speed greater than twenty-five or thirty miles an hour—in contrast to my other grandfather, Don Self, who kept in his carport Oldsmobiles and Buicks of the massive sort that easily handled ninety miles per hour on the interstate—and I remember, in some way that is as much emotional as pictorial, the scenery that characterized that part of Florida in the years before the Gulf Coast became the densely populated, semiurban landscape it is now.

Coastal Florida at that time was much as one might have imagined it, and, I suspect, much as people would have liked it—people who, like my father's family from Virginia and my mother's from Tennessee, moved south to get in on one of the miniature economic booms, which, during the forties, fifties, and sixties, spurred growth and brought jobs to the developing seaside sprawl. Florida in those long-gone days was, as I remember it, a realm of tannin-black rivers and crystal springs; of live, unpolluted oyster beds two feet under the shallow bay and estuary waters; of red tile roofs showing here and there above the royal palms and the mangrove thickets that opened onto white beaches accessible by humpbacked bridges that were always crowded, in the magic hours before sundown, with fishermen reeling in grouper, snapper, and snook. What I remember most from my early childhood in Florida is an intensity of color both in and above the water, as clouds swept eastward over the ocean, bringing afternoon showers that could begin with a few drops carried on the wind, then abruptly open up and rain down, flooding the streets, the sidewalks, the lawns and tennis courts, the entire world it seemed to me, before eventually, after little more than an hour or two, blowing inland. Often, during storms, a greenish cast of light filled the subtropical sky over Siesta Key, infusing the palm fronds and the leaves of the trees with an even brighter green, yet turning the gulf and the bay, into whose low swells gulls and pelicans were forever diving, a deep, almost olive shade that I have never seen in water anywhere else.

But what about my taciturn grandfather and his taciturn brother? Legend has it that, on a certain slow pilgrimage to Titusville or Arcadia, they pulled into one of the ubiquitous roadside places where plaster birdbaths and imitation Greek and Roman statuary got sold to migrants and retirees with delusions of grandeur. Using as few words as possible, the brothers asked the owner what he thought his inventory might be worth in cash. The owner told them that he imagined the entire stock might be worth about forty dollars. Without another word, the brothers produced the forty dollars, a twenty-dollar bill apiece, a grand amount for workingmen in the years immediately following the Second World War. They started the car and drove wordlessly down the road about a quarter mile— I don't know which of them, Robert or Frank, was at the wheel—then turned the car around, motored back up the highway, steered into the entrance to the lot, and plowed through the statues at some remarkably low velocity, destroying every one. It is hard to know how to judge this story, particularly given that neither brother was much of a talker; and so I wonder who first told about the roadside stand and their fraternal telepathy and the pulverized birdbaths, and to whom. I find the tale pleasing.

All things considered, it seems that Bob—or, I should say, Eldridge—never had optimum chances for success in life. In addition to the difficulties imposed by an eccentric father and an imperious mother, he had to contend with his older brother, my father. In stories my mother told about him, my father as a young man comes off as an intimidatingly popular and accomplished student, clearly in the most-likely-to-succeed category, and much doted on by his mother, who, removed at last to Florida, had become the Sarasota High School Latin teacher, known to her students as Old Caesar. And, in fact, Eliza Antrim had in good measure the kind of sober reserve with which urbane people carry themselves when living in environments that are essentially colonial. The same could probably have been said for Julius Caesar, keeping order by the sword in the barbarous reaches of the empire. Unlike the historical Caesar's imperial subjects, though, my grandmother's students eventually moved on in life, escaping her rule. Even my father, who, by becoming a professor, a professional intellectual, ful-filled in part her dreams for him, was able to marry, have children, and build a life separate from his mother. My uncle remained her vassal for life.

Here's some of what I know. In 1958, at the age of eighteen, Eldridge left home to study literature and art at the University of the South, in Sewanee, Tennessee. He painted and made drawings, but none of his work survives from this period, or from any other in his life. After college, he moved north to New York City, where he settled into an apartment in the East Seventies and enrolled in the Manufacturers Hanover Trust executive-training program. It is unlikely that he had plans to support himself as an artist by becoming a bank vice-president. Apparently, he accumulated debts, spent evenings in the bars along Second and Third avenues, and either failed or simply dropped out of the training program, though not before meeting, in his classes on retail and commercial banking, the love of his life. M. was—and is—a beautiful and intelligent woman who remained until recently a successful banker. The fact that my uncle became, subsequent to his rapid exit from corporate culture, a cabdriver and an Upper East Side doorman did not deter M., who undoubtedly saw, as people will when profoundly attached to lovers on their way to falling through the cracks, some version of him that would forever exist as Potential.

I remember M. from a trip my family took to New York when I was ten and my sister nine; and I remember my uncle in his apartment, a place I thought of frequently when I found myself living in New York, in my own small, sparsely furnished walk-up only blocks away from where he'd lived twenty years before. The highlight of that trip was an afternoon at FAO Schwarz, the world's greatest toy store, gift certificates—presents from Uncle Eldridge—clutched in our hands. I chose, after much exploring and considering (and perhaps in awareness that it was my uncle's dream to get his pilot's license and fly jumbo jets), one of those plastic planes driven by a loud, buzzing engine in circular orbit around the "pilot." It was a cheap toy airplane destined to crash and break apart when, as soon as my father got it in the air (I never flew the thing), the handheld control lines became tangled and useless, causing the plane to jerk downward and nose-dive into the ground.

At any rate, M. was very much on the scene at that time, and my sister and I pestered her and Eldridge mercilessly about their getting married—why weren't they *married?*—much as we would hound them about this in the years to come, even after our uncle had given up on New York and drifted down the coast, finally returning to Florida to live in his parents' house, in a tiny wood-paneled room crammed with guns and ammunition, British novels, all manner of sporting gear, antique toy soldiers displayed on dusty shelves, a short and narrow bed with a tartan blanket, and, stacked within easy reach of the bed, back issues of the same kinds of magazines he kept in the trunk of his car—automobile, airplane, scuba, golf, tennis, rifle, archery, and *Playboy*.

It may have been his room that attracted me, when I was a teenager in Miami, to my uncle's way of life. Everything about it seemed desirable to me, because it was *his*, I suppose, and because everything he did spoke to adolescent pleasures.

He created the illusion that he was his own man, and free.

I was thirteen when I started riding the bus across the Everglades to visit him. I used to sit by the window and watch for alligators in the black canals beside the highway, as, in the far distance, fires lit by heat lightning burned off the dry grass and the stunted pines that grew in clusters like innumerable tiny islands rising from the shallow waters south of Naples. By this time, around 1972, my grandfather Robert Antrim had died, and my uncle had more or less abandoned any dreams he might have had of a life somewhere removed from his mother's house. My own mother's drinking had reached a level best described as operatically suicidal, and she and my father—married, divorced, then remarried to each other—waged their war nightly. My sister had got busy saving herself through academics. I'd got busy flunking out. Our Siamese had eaten a poisonous South American toad and was afflicted with seizures that caused her to fall down and twitch violently. The other cat had reached the age at which vomiting was chronic.

And when in the deep of the night my mother came into my room swaying, half conscious and with gray smoke from her cigarette wreathing her face, shattered by bourbon and white wine; and when she raised her hand to strike, and I easily batted her arm back, then stepped forward and quickly steadied her before she tipped; when, holding my mother upright, I looked past her to see my father watching us from the shadows outside my room, whispering that he was sorry for everything—when these things happened, there eventually came a point at which feeling, or whatever it is we call feeling, broke apart in me. And though it's true that I felt anger and shame and fear—emotions that I live with still, more than thirty years after my solitary pilgrimages to the playtime world of Uncle Bob—it was also true that I felt nothing at all. And in order to share this feeling that was not a feeling, in order to be with another person, a man, as I realize now, who was like the man I might one day become, a man drained of feeling, I boarded a bus.

The bus carried me past Frog City and the Miccosukee Indian settlements, all those alligator-wrestling parks and airboat-rental outposts. At Naples, the scenery changed, and the bus took a right turn and headed up the suburban Gulf Coast, stopping in Fort Myers, Punta Gorda, Port Charlotte, and other centerless non-towns I can't remember the names of, continuing north toward Venice, the home of retired circus performers, crossing one bridge after another and another, over narrow inlets and motorboats moored by the hundreds, before finally arriving, after what seems in memory an endless journey, in Sarasota, the town where I was born, and where my uncle, sunburned and smelling of English Leather and the beer he'd drunk the night before, waited to greet me at the station with the one question I have been trying to answer for myself ever since: "What do you want to do?"

We got in the car. We rolled down the windows. We turned on the radio. We began to drive. After a moment, I asked him the question I always looked forward to asking upon seeing him for the first time in a long time.

"Eldridge, what are you eating?"

"Pork chops."

"How're you fixing them?"

"I'm broiling them."

"What are you having with them?"

"Spinach."

"What else?"

"Rice."

Or:

"String beans."

Or:

"Fries."

It worked out, he would explain—and my uncle was forced to explain this again and again, because people loved hearing it—that, over the course of a year, eating a menu that consisted of one entrée per month (scallops in March; spaghetti in April; flounder in May), he got a balanced diet.

It is easy, looking back on all this now, to appreciate the despair and the terror inherent in my uncle's preoccupations with self-sufficiency and preparedness, at home and in his car— particularly in the car, a four-door gas guzzler not unlike a rent-a-wreck version of the cars my mother's father drove, a car different in every respect from the one that had, at a certain moment in my uncle's youth, defined his enthusiasm for life. That car was a sexy, cherry-red Triumph TR3 with a walnut steering wheel and a rusted-out hole in the passenger-side floor—a casualty of salt air and the Florida weather—which forced the passenger to position himself extremely carefully, especially since the Triumph's chassis rode quite low to the road. I was only seven or eight years old when Eldridge took me for drives in that car. As he accelerated and the RPM needle flickered on the dash, I would lean carefully forward and to the left, reaching, at my uncle's invitation, to take hold of the wheel and guide the car along a straight path down the Sarasota streets.

But back to the story of Eldridge and his things. Each morning, he went to the carport and opened the trunk of the car. He stood before the items stowed there, moving and shifting his gear, replacing sweaty tennis clothes with clean ones, improving the overall packing dynamics, while, inside the house his white-haired mother, who often stayed up all night pacing, padded from bedroom to living room to porch to kitchen, worrying whether her son and grandson might eat a little breakfast before abandoning her for a day of horsing around and playing tennis and shooting pool with the friends from the Canada Dry loading dock out by the airport.

Once he'd established that everything was in order, that we had whatever we might need if, say, the world were to blow up and all life outside our car were to be catastrophically extinguished, we were off and running. Of what were our days together made? Looking back, I would say that our days were made of desire. We had structured activities, like tennis— I had not yet wrecked my shoulder with my high-toss, low-percentage, erratic yet explosive service, the theatrical serve of a flailing boy—and less formal pastimes, like wandering into convenience stores for supplies, crossing one of the crowded bridges leading to Siesta Key and the beach, driving north and dropping in at Joel's house, stopping over afterward at Roger's. There always came that point in tennis when the black clouds appeared from the gulf, and the rain came down, and everyone bolted off the courts and drank water. Then, just as suddenly, the sky would clear, and the world would become loud with the sounds of seagulls calling and smaller birds chattering. The sun would emerge, and we'd pick up mid-game, aiming to avoid puddles. After the game, we would walk out to the parking lot and my uncle would open the trunk of his car.

The trunk, as I see it now, was a physical repository, a form of warehouse or armory, in which my uncle secreted aspects of himself that would become, as the years went by, forbidden, denied, historical, forgotten. The things in the trunk were symbols of whatever in our lives—his and mine—might one day be taken away, totems representing sex and sport, music and work, eating and drinking, even talking and laughing. Together, my uncle and I stood in the parking lot with our hands in our pockets, staring at the pieces of the life we desired; and occasionally I would reach in and remove something, an article of clothing, for instance, or Eldridge's disassembled fishing rod in its case. I might hold and admire the object, then put it back in its place, after which Eldridge would close the trunk and we would walk around to the sides of the car, open the doors, and get in. Our conversations were perfect. Whenever I said to him, in language sometimes having to do with home, sometimes with school, that I wanted to escape my situation, he nodded and suggested that we drive out to Siesta Key and have a swim at the beach before the sun went down.

The last day I ever spent with him, we played doubles with Roger and Joel. From the courts we could see Sarasota Bay and, lit violet against the red sunset, the shell-shaped roof of the Van Wezel Performing Arts Hall, known because of its paint job as the Purple Cow. After the game, my uncle and I walked to the car. As usual, we peered into, rummaged through, and slammed shut the trunk. Possibly I asked Eldridge about M. Had she been to visit? Was she coming? Did he love her? Did she love him? Would they ever get married? Why not? Then we drove to Joel's house, in a development near Bradenton. Immediately after we'd walked in the front door, the telephone rang. Joel's wife answered, put the phone down on a counter, and said, "Bob, it's your mother. She's been calling."

It happened frequently. Within a few hours of our leaving the house, his mother began dialing numbers for bars, restaurants, people's homes, wherever he might be found. She wanted to know when he planned to return to her. She wanted to know if he was drinking beer. She wanted to know if he would be out late. She wanted to know if he was telling her the truth. I could hear him speaking into the phone in Joel's kitchen, answering her: "Yes, Don's here. Yes, he's having a good time. No, I'm not letting him drink any beer. Yes, he's had something to eat. No, I'm not driving fast. No, we won't be out late." So it went. When we left Joel's and drove with Roger and Joel and Joel's wife in a caravan to shoot pool on the enormous pool table that happened to be pretty much the only item of furniture in Roger's living room—in Roger's entire house, as far as I could make out—the telephone rang and again I heard my uncle speaking to my grandmother:

"Yes, we're playing pool. No, we're not betting any money. Don't worry, I won't let him drink any beer. Yes, we'll be home soon."

It was around this time that I was learning, in imitation of my uncle's adult friends, to call Eldridge Bob.

"Bob, what are we eating?" I asked him when, later that night, after tennis and billiards, after we'd driven out Fruitville Road to the house, parked in the carport, and checked the trunk one last time, we left the world of the car and entered the realm of Eldridge and his mother.

The stove lights were on in the kitchen. On the other side of the house my grandmother moved about. I could see her in

49

the shadows. She was a pale shadow in her blue housedress in her dark bedroom, behind sliding glass doors that opened through curtains onto the porch, where I slept on a sofa bed.

"Pork chops."

"What are we having with them?"

"Fries."

"All right. Is it time for Johnny Carson?"

"Just about."

"Should I turn on the TV?"

"Turn it on," he said. He was cooking, using the broiler and a fork. I sat in his room, where the TV was, staring at his magazines. My uncle, I remember, always had in his room a certain game for one player, Labyrinth, basically a wooden box fitted with a pivoting top, on which was fashioned a kind of maze through which the player maneuvered a steel ball. My uncle could turn the knobs and guide the ball safely through. I drank a soda and played the game for a while, and my uncle opened another beer for himself.

Eldridge was a tall and beautiful-looking man. He tanned in the sun to a reddish shade characteristic among people of Scottish descent. His forehead had a scar from the time he'd walked straight into a forklift blade. His beer gut did not detract from his appeal. He wore a gold chain. He looked as if he'd be right at home at the Playboy Mansion pool parties pictured in the magazines beside the bed.

Johnny Carson came on the television. We ate with our plates balanced on our laps. My uncle blanketed his pork chops beneath a layer of pepper. I did the same. The pork chops were dry and hard, and the pepper bounced off them. The television's reception was fuzzy; its antenna had to be adjusted periodically. I was aware that I wanted to be like my uncle, aware as well that I wasn't so sure about that. I complained to him about my father, who had begun to worry absurdly over my prospects, if I kept going the way I was going, for graduate school. Sometimes, when I complained, Bob taunted me for not having the courage to drop out of school altogether. I must have felt, somehow, that my uncle and his brother had, throughout their lives, been at odds with each other. Bob and I watched Carson host guest after guest. In my memory, this was the night that the comedian Steve Martin came on and stole the show with a cheap prop arrow sticking through his head. Or was it the night that Martin came out and did the half-a-beard routine?

I put my plate down, got up, and walked through the open glass doors to the sunporch. I heard Bob in his room, undressing. After a moment he came out and stood beside my sofa bed. He was wearing boxer shorts and a T-shirt, and he was making fun of me, but the joking had now passed the point at which it was pleasurable, because he had drunk so much.

I was standing beside the bed. He was standing beside me. He pushed me gently, and suddenly we were falling. We were wrestling on the bed. He climbed on top of me, and I squirmed beneath him. I was on my stomach and my uncle was on my back. He had my arms pinned. His movements were sluggish. We were wrestling, and then we were no longer wrestling. He forced me to stay still and be quiet. I could smell the salty, burned scent of his skin; and I could smell the warm beer on his breath as he exhaled against the side of my face. He stopped moving, and I stopped moving.

He breathed.

I breathed.

He was spread across me. His chest pressed me down into the bed. His face was next to mine.

How long did we stay like that, breathing together on the folded-out sofa? The moment did not last long. The time that elapsed was the time it took for our friendship to end. Had he passed out? Was he waiting for me to speak? Was it safe to move? I felt the dead weight of him on me, and my feelings about him, and about his way of life, changed. I perceived that this man on top of me was a drunk in his underwear, a man who ate the same food night after night in a room in his mother's house, and I was terrified.

"Get up," I told him. He lifted himself. He got off me. I watched him rise and walk unsteadily in bare feet to his room. The lights in his room went dark. I heard the springs squeaking inside his little bed; and I thought I saw, in the hours before I fell asleep, his mother, my grandmother, pacing behind the curtains drawn behind the glass doors leading to her room at the far end of the house. There had been a time, when I was little, that I had slept in her bed with her. But the far end of the house seemed to me, that night, after Eldridge had gone to bed, like a truly faraway place.

The next morning I told my uncle I had to leave Sarasota. I didn't say why, and I don't know whether he, in some way, understood. I just told him I had to go. He drove me to the station. He put me on a bus, and I rode the bus down the Tamiami Trail, stopping at the towns along the way, traveling south past Naples, southeast across the Everglades. After a long ride I saw, through the bus windows on the right, the enormous cement factory that, in those days, marked the end of the journey home.

When I was sixteen, I left Miami for boarding school in the foothills of the Blue Ridge Mountains. Two years after that, I went north to college, and four years later I moved to New York, where I still live. During these years I saw my uncle only a handful of times. My mother, in the decade after she got sober, in 1983, made an effort to stay in touch with him. At some point, he and my grandmother moved from their house to a small apartment. It was in this apartment that Eliza died, and he was left alone. For years, he worked as a prep cook in a restaurant on Siesta Key. He used to go in late, after the restaurant had closed, and work until dawn, preparing and organizing food for the cooks who came in mornings to make lunch. My uncle liked this routine, because it protected him from ever having to see or talk to another person. He told my mother that he didn't think he could go to AA and stop drinking, because he was afraid that his anger, were he not medicated by alcohol, might cause him to harm someone.

At the age of fifty-two, he died. My mother told me later that his weight had dropped precipitously, that he'd turned yellow, that, at the end, he'd bled through his skin. And she told me a story about the last year of his life, a story about a woman no one in our family had known a thing about.

Back when he was a boy, back in that ancient time when Robert Antrim was driving over birdbaths and urns, Eldridge had known a girl who lived on a farm that neighbored his mother's brother Tom's property on the James River, near Amherst, Virginia. My uncle and this girl had ridden horses to-

53

gether. The girl fell in love with Eldridge, and she never forgot him. Like Eldridge, she grew up to live a difficult life in which she became an alcoholic and found herself alone in the world. In the year before he died, she somehow tracked him down. She came to Sarasota to be with him for whatever time they had left. She tried to get him to eat, and she measured out what he could drink. She was dying herself, of a brain tumor. She was there—ensconced in the apartment my uncle had shared with his mother—when, in 1992, my mother drove to Sarasota to say good-bye to her ex-husband's brother, whom she liked to refer to, in the spirit of the old days, as Sam. The story goes that, at the moment Sam died, this woman none of us knew, who was alone in the apartment, saw—so she later reported to my mother, an ideal audience—bloody footprints walk across the living-room floor.

I never know what to make of these kinds of stories, or of the people who tell them. The truth of the matter is that I neither believe nor wholly discount the tale of the bloody footprints, in part because I think Eldridge should be allowed a memorable parting gesture, a gesture of—what? Loneliness? The woman from Virginia became the custodian of his ashes, which she carried home to Virginia with her. Shortly after that, she, too, died. My mother told me, years later, that this woman from the farm on the river in the foothills of the Blue Ridge had had a brother, a man who lived deep in the woods, and who was rumored to be a violent person. My mother supposed that Eldridge's ashes might have fallen into the hands of this man.

After his brother's death, my father drove up the Tamiami Trail to Sarasota and cleared out the apartment. There was no funeral. I asked my father what had become of Eldridge's rifles and his records, his scuba and golf and tennis gear, and he told me that these things had been replaced by high-caliber handguns and case after unopened case of small-arms ammunition, which he, my father, had dug out of the bedroom closet and hauled back to the gun shop, where he'd convinced the owner to buy them back.

PART III

n the fall of 1988, six years after the close of my parents'
second marriage, four years before the death of Eldridge,
my mother telephoned from Miami to inform me that her
boyfriend, S., whom she had met in Alcoholics Anonymous,
would soon be en route to New York. The reason for S.'s
visit—his first since the mid-seventies, when, as a young man
setting out to study painting and drawing, he'd fallen instead
into drinking, and become, according to my mother, at least
intermittently itinerant—was, my mother told me, to locate
and, with any luck, authenticate a certain painting, a landscape
that had, back when S. was an aspiring artist living in Manhattan, captivated his imagination.

"Painting? Authenticate?" I asked.

"He'll have to tell you about it. It's his trip," she told me.
Then she said, "Hang on a minute," and there was a rustling
sound—my mother's open hand closing over the telephone's
mouthpiece—and I could hear her saying to S., in a stage whis-
per that revealed the faint nasality of her southern-Appalachian
accent, "Go ahead and tell Don what you need to tell him.
He'll listen."

S. spoke exceedingly slowly and quietly. I stood in the
cramped and cluttered kitchen of the Upper East Side apart-

ment that I shared, in those days, with my girlfriend, K. I pressed the phone receiver against my ear and heard S.'s soft, anxious voice, a voice made, as I think of it now, almost entirely of breath, of exhalations, saying, at the excruciating rate of about one word every ten seconds—I am exaggerating in fact, though not in spirit—"Oh,

hello,

     Don."

"What's up?" I said.

"Not

    much,

       I

          suppose."

"Mom says you're coming to New York," I said quickly, trying to use my own words the way an English bobby uses his nightstick to hurry vagrants along.

"New York . . . ," he said.

And I waited.

". . . Yes . . . ," he went on.

We waited. And eventually, gradually, infuriatingly, in bits and pieces, a story emerged—the story of the painting.

The painting, I learned, was old. It was rectangular in shape, maybe four feet tall and two feet wide. Its wooden frame was large and slightly ornate. As I understood things, the work belonged—or had once belonged—to a man who owned a brownstone in Chelsea, a boardinghouse, a building in which men lived in rooms. It is possible that this man had bought the painting somewhere in Europe or America. Or maybe he had simply found it.

Slowly, over the course of many minutes, my mother's

boyfriend in Miami told me that there had been another man on the scene in the downtown boardinghouse. For some reason, I am under the impression that this man was related to a friend of S.'s; he was, I believe, one of several cousins who at one time or another either had possession of or claimed to know something about the painting. Anyway, this man remembered having seen, in an art magazine, a reproduction of the work. The cousin could not recall the name or the date of the magazine or even the content of the article. In fact, all the cousin remembered with any certainty, according to S., was the fact that the painting was "important."

But in what way important? This was the question that was to become—*had* become—S.'s obsession.

For nearly fifteen years after he left New York, my mother told me, S. had wandered up and down the Eastern Seaboard, living in short-term lodgings, drinking, and working the kinds of temporary jobs—auto-body painting, sign painting, construction, and so on—that are often performed by people in his situation. At a certain point, he wound up back in Florida, where he was from, and where, after repeated attempts—in this he was like my mother; the movement from defeat to recovery was a bond between them—he had managed to get, and stay, sober. He had even begun, for the first time since dropping out of the School of Visual Arts in New York, to paint.

I have one of S.'s paintings from this period hanging on my living-room wall. Like all the works he made after joining AA and moving into my mother's condominium in South Miami, it is signed with his middle name, Craig. It is small, more or less the size and shape of an LP record jacket, and it is, as were many of S.'s works, a landscape. But it is not painted from life.

Or is it? It shows, in the middle distance, and to the right side, a steep-sided mountain, predominantly white and lavender in color, as if overgrown with flowering plants. In the upper-left foreground (hanging down from a corner, like decorative proscenium elements) are some delicately painted leaves that look almost prehistoric; far off to the right, against the mountain and a blue-white-lavender sky, a solitary, impossibly tall and narrow palm tree seems to be growing out of an impossibly deep and wide gorge. When I look at the painting, with its strange topography, its sliver of moon in an unnatural sky, and its dizzying, off-center palm tree, I feel there is something amiss in the relative sizes and positions of the objects. The effect is of a disturbance, either in the mind of the painter or in the world of the painting. And I feel, considering this disturbance, that the scene is missing something—a *Tyrannosaurus rex*, perhaps. Then I notice, in a way that has more to do with feeling than observation, the symmetry inside the disturbance, and I am aware that S., deliberately and skillfully, or maybe by accident, has painted a truly alternative world, which is to say a world that is different from ours not only by virtue of the imaginary elements of which it is composed but also in the laws of whatever nature governs the spatial relations between those elements.

But what about the other painting, the one from S.'s days as a young artist living in New York? For S., that painting had been, during his transient years, a source of creative contemplation, and a symbol of whatever remained in him of the will to escape his circumstances and work as an artist. More to the point—and especially during the period when he was, to use an expression that is popular in AA rooms everywhere, hitting bottom—it had, I believe, served as a symbol, maybe *the* spiritual symbol, of his desire to live. He had thought about, and pondered over, that painting almost every day of his life as an alcoholic. When he was spraying paint on rusted cars, when he was hammering carpentry nails, when he was sitting at a bar, in New York or Florida, he thought about the painting. S. thought about the man who had first suggested the importance of the work, and about the magazine article that he had heard about but never seen; and these thoughts led him to think about European and American painting traditions, and about the history of art in general, and, I suppose, about all the famous paintings that he had seen only in books. The memory of the important painting in its huge and heavy wooden frame—not to mention a preoccupation with the thought of one day verifying his evolving ideas about the painting's provenance—had, I realized in my conversations with both S. and my mother, helped keep him alive.

"What do you think it is?" I finally asked him at some point in our phone conversation, that day in 1988.

"Well,

    I

        think

            it's

          a

               da Vinci."

"A what?" I said.

". . . a Leonardo da Vinci," he said.

"Put Mom on the phone, okay?" I said.

"Hello? Don?"

"What's going on?"

"He believes the painting may be a Leonardo da Vinci, dear."

"I know. I heard him."

"He's going to spend a week in New York and he wants to research this and he wants to know if you'll help."

"Help?"

Which is what I did. After a fashion. When you are, as I was—and as I am—the anxious child of a volatile, childlike mother, you learn how to appear to accept, as realistic and viable, statements and opinions that are clearly ludicrous.

You may learn, too, as a defense against the absurd disappointments caused by fragile and unhappy parents, the crude art of sarcasm. "When is he coming on this vision quest?" I asked my mother, and she filled me in on the details. A month or so later, S. took up temporary lodging with—and here the story becomes somewhat foggy—one or another of those above-mentioned cousins, the man who, following the death of the owner of the downtown boardinghouse in which S. had first seen the painting, now had possession of the painting. S. promptly photographed it, then took a pair of scissors and cut swatches from the spare canvas tucked away along the inside perimeter of the stretcher. This seemed to me to be an act of mutilation, or, at the very least, one of proprietary aggression, and probably out of keeping with whatever protocol might exist for the care of old artworks. Were you supposed to chop up the canvas? On the other hand, what concern was it of mine? Why should I care what S. might do to some painting that was, in all likelihood, just a piece of junk sitting in an apartment?

Questions like this—any and all questions, for that matter, concerning S., my mother, and the painting—frequently became points of division between me and K. Long before any of this crazy art-historical family business ever got started, K. had learned that whenever my mother and I got involved in each other's lives, even over matters of no apparent consequence, there was likely to be trouble on the way for her, trouble in the form of fighting between us. In those years, I was terribly unskilled at managing the consequences of my loyalty to my mother, a person who was constitutionally incapable of staying out of her children's affairs, or of coping with what she regarded as hostile infractions—"Mom, do *you* think the painting is a Leonardo da Vinci?"—against her own liberal and openminded worldview. Thus I found myself repeatedly subjecting K. to antagonistic appraisals of my mother's cultivation of fantasy. When K. went along with my negative assessments, I turned the tables on her and rushed to my mother's defense.

S., in the meantime, had arrived in Manhattan. He was coming full circle. I remember that he visited me and K. in our apartment on Eighty-fifth Street. I also have a memory of going with him to see the painting. What I chiefly remember about the painting now is not how it looked, precisely, but how I felt, standing next to my mother's boyfriend, a man on a mission to find a Leonardo da Vinci.

As I recall, the painting appeared dirty. It was leaning against a wall. Its carved and filigreed frame was, as S. had indicated, massive and even oppressive; it had the look of mahogany, stained to a shade of darker brown, that I have come to associate with the woodwork inside Victorian-era brownstones; the frame was about the size of a headboard for a bed. The painting—imprisoned, as it were, inside this boxy frame—looked somehow out of scale with itself. I should point out that at that time in my life I knew practically nothing about the history of painting, European, American, or otherwise, and that what little I know today would in no way qualify me to appraise a work of art. That said, the painting did not strike me as an Old Master. It did not, in fact, look like an obvious *find*, regardless of its period. In the bottom half of the picture was a rocky stream or small river that tumbled directly toward the viewer. Trees grew along the banks of the stream, and green hills sloped up and away from the center of the painting. The foreground was dominated, interestingly, by a number of tall and leafy marsh reeds; on the stalk of one sat a bird—in the dove family?—rendered large for the sake of perspective. The sky above this nature scene was radiant, glowing, painted in an almost white shade near the horizon, and growing, with in-creasing altitude, darker and grayer, as if the unseen sun had barely begun to rise.

But something about those round rocks and the water cas-cading over them did not look right to me. The colors, I thought, seemed odd; the trees were luridly dark, while the river was sparkling and bright. The light in the painting, the light from the invisible though rising (or possibly setting) sun, originated in the background. Wouldn't that background light argue for a darker foreground river? And what about those leafy Southern Hemisphere plants? What about the single, fat songbird? Overall, the scene looked romantic in a faintly un-pleasant way. It looked, I thought, off-puttingly Victorian—as did the frame. I couldn't help thinking of turn-of-the-century stained glass. I did not find the work beautiful.

And yet I have to admit that it affected me. Whenever I think about it, I am struck by a desire to see it again.

All I have to look at, though, is the photograph S. took during his stay in New York, a badly aimed, poorly lit snapshot printed on Kodak paper. I also have a few scraps of the canvas that S. scissored off the painting's stretcher. And I have copies of the replies written to S. by curators to whom he had sent letters of inquiry and, presumably, duplicates of the photograph. One letter to S., dated November 28, 1988, and sent to my mother's address in Miami, is from the Frick Collection, and it suggests that S. contact the European Paintings Department at the Metropolitan Museum of Art. The letter is a clear blow-off. Who could blame the people at the Frick? An undiscovered Leonardo? Another letter, from the New York Public Library, proposes that S. get in touch with the Stevens Institute of Technology in Hoboken, in reference to the Leonardo da Vinci collection there. A December 9, 1988, letter from Sotheby's indicates a lack of interest in offering the work at auction.

What was S. *doing?*

In addition to posting letters to museums, he was going to the Frick Art Reference Library, on Seventy-first Street, where he spent days paging through old art books in the hope of finding a plate that matched the snapshot he carried everywhere he went. He stressed to me the value of *old* art books, reasoning that the painting—which, he theorized, had been either stolen or lost from a private collection—might have been in currency in former times. When I wondered aloud why he didn't throw the painting into a taxi and haul it straight to the Met, he made the excuse that, after all, it was not *his* painting to cart around town. Besides, he told me, he enjoyed looking through those old books in those fascinating archives, which were, I realized, a world away from suburban Miami and his life as an under-employed artist with a history of dead-end jobs.

In Miami, my mother waited for word. We spoke more and more frequently. "Have you heard any news from S. about the painting?" she'd ask me. Or I might ask her, "Have you heard any news from S. about the painting?" But I'm not sure that I ever told her, in so many words, what I thought of S. and his ideas about the painting.

"Mom, can I ask you a question?"

"Sure."

"Why doesn't he take the painting to be evaluated by some-one who knows about these things?"

"Don, this is *his* project. I think we ought to just let him do things his way. It's important to him."

"I know that. But his way isn't very productive."

"We don't know that yet."

"Well."

"This means a lot to him, and he needs to sort it out in his own good time," she told me, and I could hear, in her voice, the serene detachment so crucial to ongoing sobriety. But I also heard—and maybe this was what that detachment was meant to hide—something that sounded a lot like fear. She was, after all, S.'s partner. She was implicated in his scheme to identify what might become, if he could prove its authenticity, one of the most famous paintings in the world. My mother, in the years after she got sober, had shown an alarming gullibility in matters relating to mental and spiritual health. By 1988, I had become adept at listening to her describe workshops devoted to past-life channeling, to radical forms of astrology, to speaking in dead languages. What was her angle on the painting? Did she truly think that her boyfriend had stumbled on a Leonardo da Vinci? Or was she simply concerned about the effects on S. of what might, were he ever to actually identify the painting, come as a shattering disappointment?

And what about *me*? Why was I going along with this nonsense, phoning museums and antiquarian booksellers and dealers, and asking them, on S.'s behalf, what a person might do, in the event that such a person might or might not know about a painting that might or might not be a missing priceless European treasure?

After a handful of humiliating phone calls, I gave up. I simply couldn't do it. I wished S. well—he had by then returned to Miami—and I asked him to keep me informed of his progress. I put the snapshots he'd given me, along with the swatches of decaying brown fabric, in a drawer. And I tried to stop thinking about the problem of the painting.

One aspect of the problem, however, had me bothered. For many years, back in the days when she was drinking, my mother (in the manner of so many high-functioning alcoholics who get a lot done) had run a college department that specialized in costume history, fashion design, and textile chemistry. She knew how to date a fabric sample. Or, if she didn't know how to do it herself, she knew how to contact people who did.

I asked her about this. "Mom, does that canvas seem to you to be about five hundred years old?"

"It's so hard to tell, Don."

"What do you think?"

"I don't know."

"Can't you take a piece over to the University of Miami and see if anyone there can subject it to some tests?"

"Oh, I couldn't."

"Why not?"

"I need to respect the fact that this is not my affair."

"You don't want to find out, do you? You don't want to know!" I said to her at some point along the way.

Most likely, I was getting squared off to pick a fight with K., who, in fact, had been more than decent about this whole enterprise.

"How's your mother?" K. would sometimes ask, when she saw me stagger off the phone like a person who'd drunk from a goblet that had smoke billowing over its rim.

"They're out of their minds! They're out of their minds! Leonardo da Vinci? Fuck me!"

"Donald, you knew it was insane."

"I know."

"So what's the surprise?"

"It's not—it's not that it's a *surprise*. It's not a surprise."

"Okay? So?"

K. had a point. Unfortunately, an understanding of reality is a liability in a situation in which reality is inadmissible—or, rather, in a situation in which people's feelings and hunches, their hungers and appetites, serve as reality. Hidden inside the unfolding narrative of the painting—a narrative not only of feelings and hunches but also of grandiose hopes and dreams—was, I felt, the story of my alcoholic family. This story, now being told through the story of a moldy old painting that *might*, until shown otherwise, be a Leonardo da Vinci, was, I thought, a story in which pretty much everything that could ever happen in life—everything that could come true tomorrow, or the next day, or the day after that—might, until shown otherwise, be the miraculous, transformative thing that, like a great work of art, brings us closer to salvation.

"Your *mother*," K. would say to me whenever I got off the phone. Then she would sigh.

A few years before S. undertook his pilgrimage to the art libraries of New York, I boarded a plane and flew to Miami to visit my mother. It was a trip I had been looking forward to. In some ways, I suppose, I had been looking forward to this trip for much of my life. The time had come, my mother and I had agreed, for us to have a talk about our past. Specifically, she had invited me to sit at the table and tell her what it had been like, during the years in which she'd lived in and out of a blackout, to be her child.

It was, as I recall, the week of Thanksgiving. My grandparents were driving down from North Carolina. They, S., and I were gathering at my mother's apartment to give thanks for her relatively new sobriety, which, however insecure, had nonetheless been hard won.

A night or two before this celebration was to take place, I sat in the dining room with S. and my mother. I suppose I must have been twenty-seven years old at the time. I remember—and I should have been more savvy about these kinds of signs and portents—that the two of them sat in chairs that had been pulled out from the table and pushed hard against the dining-room wall. I, on the other hand, sat in an improvised place lacking defined coordinates—the ambiguous middle of the room. In the scene as it was set, my mother and S. were positioned like heads of state, listening, in their official capacity, to the appeals of a supplicant. But they were also a couple of nervous alcoholics with their backs to the wall, waiting to be attacked. As usual, my mother was smoking up a storm. Her ashtray, her cigarettes, her lighter, and her coffee in its bright-red mug sat close to her on the table. Somewhere in the apartment, her fluffy white cat with a skin disease was lurking.

"Don, I want you to know that I know there are things you need to say to me," she said. And I had to wonder: What was *he* doing here? She leaned forward. "You go ahead."

"Um."

"I suspect you must be upset and curious about some things."

"Yeah."

"I've got a lot of serenity in my life now, so I can hear you." She turned to S. "Isn't that right?"

"Yes,

      that's

         right."

"Do you have serenity, Don?" my mother asked me.

"I don't know. Maybe. Yes and no."

"That doesn't sound like serenity."

"I guess it's something I'll have to work on."

"You're angry."

I sighed. Things weren't getting off to a good start. I said to my mother, "Really, I just wanted to be able to say a few things."

"I'm listening."

"I was hoping we'd talk. About the way things were when Terry and I were little. When we were growing up."

But what, after all, did I want to tell her? Did I want to tell her how scary she'd looked to me when she was drunk? Did I want to tell her what it had been like to lie awake at night, waiting for the house to be quiet? Or did I want to tell her that I, her son, lived every day with the fear that I would never know how to love another person? Were these the kinds of things that a man could say to his mother? Were these the kinds of things that a man could say to his recovering-alcoholic mother while her recovering-alcoholic boyfriend was sitting beside her?

I sat in my chair. They sat in their chairs. Not one of us, I think, was serene. Everywhere on the white walls of my mother's condominium were the framed Art Deco prints that my father had bought for her, fashion illustrations by Icart and Erté, and a large series of magazine plates of the sort that had been featured in popular French publications of the early twentieth century. The plates showed women wearing improbable dresses and enormous hats, some of them walking the favored dogs of the day, borzois and other distinguished breeds. This was my mother's art. It was from a period in history, and represented a set of styles, that she loved. I now have most of it—about a dozen pieces—in my apartment in New York, wedged behind furniture, propped against walls, where it can't easily be seen. For a while, after my mother died, I tried hanging one of the Icarts, a beautiful illustration of a woman undressing in a darkened bedroom. I gave it a prominent place over a low sofa in the living room. But after a while I couldn't bear to look at it. I had to take it down and put it away.

That night in Florida, the night in the dining room, I watched my mother smoke her cigarettes and drink her coffee. Every now and then, she reached downward and made tiny come-hither motions with her hand, in the direction of the cat, which stood off in the shadows, as if uncertain whether it was safe to come all the way into the room. I had watched my mother smoke cigarettes and drink coffee my entire life. Never at night, though. At night it had been Jim Beam in a large glass.

She said to me—and I could hear, again, that nasal, southern-Appalachian sound in her voice—"Everything you want to talk about is in the past."

"I know."

"Why do you need to live in the past?"

"I'm not living in the past."

"You are. You live in the past. I've let the past go. I don't live in the past. I won't."

"I'm not asking you to."

"Don't come into *my* home and attack *my* serenity. I don't need your hostility. If you have something constructive to add to this conversation, go ahead. But if you're going to tear me down and get at me with your hostility, that's something I don't need. You want to live in the past, and you want to drag me back into all that shit. You're angry. You're angry and you're hostile."

"Wait a minute," I begged. And I went on: "In the first place, there's a difference between anger and hostility." What a mistake. My mother glared at me, and then turned away and looked at S., who, frankly, seemed terrified. She said to him, in a kind of scream, "I don't need this hatred from my own child!"

And to me she said, "You can be a supportive member of this family or you can get out of my house."

It was not long before I found myself lying on the carpet in my mother's dining room, curled up, weeping. From time to time, I looked up and saw my mother or S., or the pair of them, peering out of their bedroom on the far side of the apartment. It was as if, like the cat, they were afraid to step into the room. Were they afraid of contamination? Contamination by the Past? I was the Past. The bedroom door would open a short way, and light would spill out, and, by that light, I could distinguish their figures. My mother looked tall and imposing in her plain white housedress. S., by contrast, was small and slight and wiry, a thin man whose gestures and movements, like his voice (and the cryptic signatures he gave his own paintings, and the haphazard research methods he would use, years later, to avoid properly identifying the painting in New York), conveyed his need to remain unseen, undetected, and, like the creator of the work that became his obsession, unknown.

I do not recall precisely how things played out over the remainder of that dismal trip to Florida. Nor do I recall at what point I became certain that S. and my mother were conspiring to leave the identity of the painting a mystery. By the middle of 1989, the matter seemed to have been dropped.

Then, after what seemed a long stretch of time, I got a phone call. It was S. He said that he had something important to tell me concerning the painting, which, as it turned out, was still in the hands of one of the cousins. S. told me that he had been doing a lot of thinking about the painting. He told me that he was, by the way, grateful for my help during the months when he had worked so hard to establish the painting's authenticity. But he had been wrong, he said, wrong about the painting. After much meditation on the problem, he had come to realize why he—*we*—had failed to identify the painting. He told me that this realization had caused him much pain, and a great deal of soul-searching. He told me that the painting was not what he had taken it to be.

Of the many silences in all the conversations I had with S. in those years—the years before he fell out of AA and out of my mother's life—this seemed the longest. I held the phone to my ear. What was S. trying to tell me?

"I

    should

        have

           known

                it's

      not

     a

   da Vinci."

"Oh," I said.

"I

    think

        it's

  a

            Frederic

                Church!"

"Excuse me?"

"Frederic Church," he said again.

Frederic Church? The Hudson River School painter? Nineteenth century? Owned that Persian-style mansion over-looking the Hudson in upstate New York? Famous for his landscapes? Spent some time in South America? Painted animals and birds?

"Frederic Church," I said to S. "Thank you for telling me that." And a while later we finished our conversation and hung up.

K. and I had, by this time, moved to another, smaller, apartment on the Upper East Side. For the better part of a year, I had been depressed, and our relationship—confined, as it were, to a space far too cramped to permit either privacy or a comfortable intimacy—was beginning to unravel.

"He says he now thinks it's a Frederic Church," I told her when, later that night, she got home from work, slammed the door to our apartment, and dumped her shoulder bag on the floor.

"Whatever," K. said, capturing perfectly, I thought, the strange and sad and true essence of everything.

And, really, that should have been that. But there was more to come.

Over a year had passed since S.'s first trip north to look at the painting. Now, in early winter, he came back. For a period of months, he lived in Manhattan, in a Chelsea boardinghouse, a building, as I imagine it, similar to the one where years earlier this story had begun. It must, for S., have been something of a homecoming. Shortly before Christmas, my mother got on a plane and flew to New York for a weeklong visit. Together, she and S. camped out in his room. There was no phone; my communication with my mother was restricted to times when she could manage to fight the winter winds and get to a pay phone on the corner. Because her circulation was bad from smoking, this was a hardship for her. Also, she was beginning to have trouble walking. During the days, S. visited galleries and museum libraries. Of course, he came up with nothing.

I had thought, I remember, that this would be a good time for my mother and K. to meet. I suggested the idea to both of them. K. said she was ready to meet my mother, and my mother crowed at the thought of meeting K., whom she had spoken with on a few occasions, when I'd shoved the phone into K.'s hand and suggested that she say hello. But what was I thinking? Did I imagine that the four of us—my emphysemic mother, her passive-aggressive boyfriend, my increasingly fed-up girlfriend, and I—would go out to a restaurant and order a meal together? Did I picture us sitting down like a family and talking about Leonardo da Vinci and Frederic Church? Nothing came of it. K. and my mother never met. And before I knew it my mother had packed her bags and gone home. A while later, S. was gone, too.

This time, though, he had something to show for his trouble. Of the cousins who at one time or another had, or *had* had, some connection to the painting, two were now dead, and a third—and this was *not* the man who had read the magazine article dedicated to the important painting—had gone ahead and given the painting to S. I learned from my mother that the cousin had said to S. something along the lines of "You're the only person in the world crazy enough to give a damn about the thing. Take it."

"What is he going to do with it?" I asked my mother during one of our long-distance phone calls. This was sometime in—I'm guessing—late 1990 or early 1991.

"I don't know, Don. He says he's going to put it in fine-art storage. He says he doesn't know what else to do with it."

"Does he still believe it's a Frederic Church?"

"You'd have to ask him."

In the summer of 1991, I moved out of the apartment I shared with K., and began a period of bouncing from place to place. For a while, I lived in a small rented room. At about this time, down in Miami, S. packed up and left my mother's apartment. My mother told me later that he had begun drinking again; he wasn't, according to her, in good shape. She bumped into him every now and then at AA meetings—he seemed to be in and out of the program—or spoke with him on the telephone. She said, in one conversation, that he had taken a job matching house-paint colors for a paint and hardware store. On another occasion, she told me that he was working as a sign painter. She did not have an address for him, but she believed that he was living somewhere out on Miami Beach. At one point, she told me that she thought he might be sleeping in his car. In the event, S. did not, she said, look as if he was getting much to eat. He was drunk a lot, drunk even when attending AA. He looked bad. She did not expect him to live long. She did not expect to see him around much, as time went on.

The matter of the painting was, as far as I was concerned, now dropped in earnest. One day, though, I got a phone call—yet another update—from my mother. It seemed, as I remember the story from her, that S. had gone to a bar on Miami Beach where he fell into conversation with a pair of foreign men, or maybe it was just one man. The men, or man, claimed to have connections to art dealers abroad, perhaps in Holland. After a while, S. got up his nerve and pulled out the photograph of the painting. I had the impression, listening to my mother, that S. did not explain his ideas about the identity of the painting; rather, he dug the picture out of his wallet, handed it over, and waited for a response. The response was one of amazement. Where had S. found this picture? Had he taken it himself? Where was the painting? Had S. *seen* the painting? Did he know its whereabouts? Did he realize the importance of this find?

According to my mother, the men informed S. that this was, without a doubt, a work by the American painter Frederic Church. It had, S. had told her, belonged to a collection in Europe, and had gone missing in the early years of the century, possibly between the wars, and had been presumed destroyed. This was what she reported to me.

"Jesus!" I said to my mother that day on the phone.

"How about that?" she exclaimed, as if the matter of the painting were now settled.

I said, "Are you serious? Do you believe any of this? What's he going to do with the painting? Where is it? Is it still in *storage*? What kind of storage? One of those outdoor *sheds*? Is the shed *waterproof*, I hope? Wait a minute. Does the painting *belong* to him? Is it *insured*? Did whoever it was in the bar say anything about its *value*? What bar was it? How do we know that any of this is for real? A *Church*? I can't believe it's a Church. Shit. What else did S. say?"

"I don't know. I don't know the answers to any of your questions. All I know is what I've told you," my mother said, and I said, speaking of S., "How in the world is he going to cope with this?"

"I've told you, I don't know, Don."

"Is he living out on the Beach?"

"I think so."

"Is he drinking?"

"Yes."

"I'm sorry."

"I know you are. I am, too."

"There's nothing to be done?"

"Don, I've done everything I can do. He's in God's hands now. He's in God's hands."

In August 1992, Hurricane Andrew struck the southern tip of Florida, with winds measured as category four. The storm tore its way through Miami, causing billions of dollars in damage. My mother's condominium was ripped apart—one whole wall was effectively dismantled and removed by the winds that rushed in from the Atlantic Ocean. All across the neighborhoods in which I had lived as a teenager, streets, homes, and businesses were wrecked.

My mother told me that the storage facility in which S. had deposited his Frederic Church—I had, I realize now, come to think of the painting as belonging to S.; and, with this in mind, and on the strength of hearsay evidence transmitted through channels that I knew from long experience to be unreliable (S. and my mother), had come to regard the painting as a genuine Church—the storage facility, as I was saying, was, according to my mother, very badly damaged. There was, I recall my mother telling me, no hope that anything would or could be left of the painting. For years, I imagined that it had been annihilated. It had been swept out to sea, or blown up the coast, or drowned in the marshlands of the Everglades.

But was that true? Was the painting really gone?

In the summer of 2003, I made an attempt to find S. I assumed he'd passed away, though I did not know for certain. My search led me to a former employer of his in Miami, the owner of a sign-painting business, who believed that S. was alive. But he did not know where, or how, to locate him. And then—suddenly—I received a message from S., leaving a number in Florida where he could be contacted. I'd called him, and he told me that he was getting his life together again, after thirteen years of drinking. In that time, he had moved up and down the East Coast and had rarely had a proper mailing address or a phone. He had heard only the day before about my mother's death. We talked for a long time, remembering her, and then he set me straight on a few matters regarding the painting, which, as it turned out, had been water-damaged but not destroyed. He had given it away, he told me, to a former friend, a bartender, who, he believed, had in turn given it to his parents in Connecticut. "It had been haunting me for a quarter of a century. I figured that was enough," S. said. I noticed that his speech was less halting than it used to be, his voice firmer.

And the painting's identity? S. had indeed met, in a Miami bar, a Belgian whose father in Antwerp had some connection with the art business. The father in Antwerp, upon seeing S.'s photograph of the painting, had inquired into its whereabouts. According to S., the Belgians offered cash for the painting. A meeting was set up. S. told me, though, that the father in Antwerp never properly identified the painting. Something about these Belgians spooked S. The meeting didn't take place. S. was left with the feeling that the Belgians knew something they weren't saying. He told me that he even went so far as to contact the State Department about them. How my mother had decided that the painting had been definitively verified as a Church, S. could not imagine.

And there was one more thing. I had always pictured S., upon first taking possession of the painting in New York, removing it from its stretcher and carrying it in a tube on the plane to Miami. In fact, the painting had been smuggled to Florida by a stewardess, an acquaintance of S.'s, who hauled it *in its frame* on board an airplane, where, unable to cram the thing into the coat closet, she locked it, against FAA regulations, in a rear lavatory. "She handed it to me in the airport, after we landed," S. told me. When I asked him if he had gone back to his own art, he told me that he had. I wished him Godspeed, and we rang off.

In early 2003, before I'd ever dreamed of hearing from S. again, I went to Paris. It was the middle of winter, and unseasonably cold. As a result, I spent most of my time indoors. One place I went for warmth was the Louvre. Because of the weather, and because, I suppose, tourism had fallen off in anticipation of the war in the Middle East, the museum was unusually empty, and it was possible to march right up to the *Mona Lisa*. Until then, I had seen this painting only in photographs; now, standing before the real article, I was struck not only by its beauty but by its oddness. I was taken, in particular, with the way in which the landscape recedes, in balanced, serpentine patterns, behind the figure of the Mona Lisa. It is a distant, verdant landscape, viewed from what appears to be an elevation; looking at the painting, it is difficult to judge, with certainty, the exact spatial relationships between the background and foreground elements. The Mona Lisa herself, though framed by this background landscape that seems to lie far away and far below—I picture her, for no good reason, sitting high on a battlement—nonetheless exists less in relation to the immediate and visible countryside than to some larger world, the world of which the painted landscape is merely a small part. Thus the figure, looking toward the viewer and away from the background vista, occupies a position in the painting that is central in more ways than one, a position defined not only by the optical perspectives that control the painting as a whole but by a subtly disorienting perspective that feels, for want of a better word, spiritual. Standing in front of the *Mona Lisa*, I thought of S.'s landscapes—the one he'd painted, which was hanging in my living room; and the supposed Church, which at that time I thought was gone forever. In both paintings, I realized, the physical perspectives are destabilizing, to the extent that the viewer is asked to communicate—visually—with the artist in a way that is not, in essence, only visual. During the years when S. was traveling to and from New York, I'd asked myself what had prompted him to consider the landscape in the giant frame a Leonardo. Of course, in asking this question I was only a question or two away from other questions, questions having to do not with paintings or with painting techniques but with the ways in which painting techniques had become the vehicles for S.'s fantasies and delusions.

But what if I had asked, instead, a different kind of question? What had S. *seen* in a Leonardo da Vinci, even in a reproduction, that had led him to imagine the world (or, at least, the world represented in paintings) as a place where even formal perspectives become wholly subjective, private creations; a place where even a realist landscape—a simple and apparently

84

straightforward depiction of the straightforwardly known world—can utterly disorient us and, in our momentary disorientation, cause us to see into worlds governed by laws other than those we rely on as somehow universal, worlds that are, in effect, governed by the traumas and hopes of others?

The question is not easily answered. S. loved my mother, and my mother loved S. She loved him for his spirit, as he tried to survive and to make, in his own paintings, and in his relationship with her, a world that looked like the world he longed for. She loved him in spite of, and because of, his preoccupation with da Vinci and with Church, his grand lost cause.

Recently, I showed the photograph of the painting to a friend, an art historian. This person seemed to think that the painting in the photograph was likely not a Church. But then she said, "You know, wait a minute. Church spent time in South America, right? He painted animals and birds into his landscapes. Could this be an oil study from his time in South America? A study for a larger work?"

That could be. I don't know. I suppose I'll have to wait for the phone to ring, and hear what comes over the line.

PART IV

O ne evening in 2003, while I was walking down a set of stairs at the New York Public Library, it occurred to me, as it had on occasions in the past, that there are people in the world who believe in an afterlife, and people who don't; and that Heaven and Hell—or whatever vague and nebulous realms exist (or don't) beyond our consciousness of them or our ability to comprehend their natures—may (or may not) be populated, as it were, with the souls of those who, during their time among the living, fell into the first category, the category of people who believe.

My mother trusted in her afterlife to come. I am not certain that I can make, on my own behalf, unambivalent claims as to the transmigration of souls. Life after death? I do admit that late one night after her father died, in 1995, I had a strong feeling that he had stopped to pay me a visit. For a few moments, I thought of him in his car, parked beside the curb outside my building in Brooklyn. The car, as I pictured it, was running—headlights and taillights on. It was October, and exhaust clouded behind the back bumper. Was my grandfather waiting for me to climb out of bed and come downstairs to say goodbye? Was he offering me a ride? I felt him near me. But I did not get up and go to the window. I did not see him (or his car), and I did not converse with his spirit. What does it mean to feel—or to imagine feeling—the silent presence of someone who has died?

From time to time, I speak to my mother. I am in the habit of occasionally filling her in on my news, explaining some problem or other that has me bothered, or maybe setting her straight, once and for all, on one of our long-standing, unresolved disputes. That is what I was doing, that evening several years ago, as I walked down the stairs at the Public Library: I was speaking (in a suitably quiet voice) to my dead mother. And it occurred to me, as I descended the massive Vermont marble stairwell at the northern end of the Humanities and Social Sciences Library, at Forty-second Street and Fifth Avenue, that it was, after all, I who was speaking to my dead mother, and not she who was speaking to me. Back in the winter of 2001, several months after her death, I spent a sleepless night imagining, in a way that felt like believing, that my mother was *inside* the expensive mattress I had bought as solace for myself in my grief. In my panic that night, I imagined her reaching up with her arms to pull me down into my new bed, wanting me to join her in death. Since that time, however, I have never experienced anything that I could call a direct communication from her. She does not summon me, as they say, from the beyond, or make her presence in the ether palpable. I do not feel her beside me in a room, or turn suddenly and, glancing over my shoulder, catch a glimpse of—her, not there.

And so I wonder: If, when it comes to life after death, I am not (exactly) a believer, why am I talking? Who do I think I'm speaking to?

When I'm talking to my mother—at home, or out on the

street, or in public buildings—there invariably comes a moment when I feel I can imagine her hovering in the near-distance, usually at a modest height above the ground, just as angels in classical paintings float in the vicinity of the upper corners of their frames. And in the instant in which I imagine her this way—less as an apparition than as a memory, in which she is sometimes a young and attractive version of herself, though more often she is older, and sick, and close to her death—I see not only her face, with her mouth curving mischievously upward at the sides, creating the dimples that accompanied her laughter or a smile; and her eyes, which typically, as they did in life, wear a look of slight bewilderment, as if everything in the world were too much for her to take in; and her weak Appalachian chin, the chin that I, too, inherited from our Scottish and English ancestors; and her hair, which, late in her life, looked as if it had been speedily cut with dull shears. I see these things, and then I see the rest of the picture. I see what she is wearing. I see, for one dreadful moment, my mother's clothes.

In particular, I see a garment that she made during the early 1990s. She was living in Miami at the time, operating a small storefront boutique that was intended as a showcase for her own increasingly eccentric fashion designs, but which was dedicated mainly to routine tailoring and alteration jobs. She never got much business. The shop was in a run-down strip mall in an underpopulated district crisscrossed with freeway overpasses, not far from the Miami River. Because the shop was not—nor would it ever be—profitable, my mother relied on her father, who lived in North Carolina, to cover the rent.

I visited the shop in 1993. I was thirty-five. Ten years had passed since my mother's last alcoholic collapse. My father was living with his new wife in southwest Miami. My sister had moved far away from South Florida to the Pacific Northwest and begun her own family. And I was living alone in Brooklyn. My mother, with help from the insurance company and her father, had relocated from a condominium that had been torn apart by Hurricane Andrew, the year before, to a one-bedroom apartment with partial views of the Miami River. And she had opened her shop. Its name was Peace Goods.

I remember that the storefront itself was tiny, and the larger building housing it cheaply constructed. I can't recall the businesses adjacent to my mother's. Was there a liquor store? In front of her shop was the parking lot. I remember her being afraid of the people who walked past her door. Her space was, as I recall, brightly lit. The air-conditioning stayed on high. Carpeting was glued to the floor. In the rear of the shop were sewing machines. A tailor's dummy—or were there two?—half-dressed in one of my mother's raw-silk works in progress, stood beside a large worktable on which she spread and cut fabric. Scissors lay ready for her to pick up, along with spooled threads, sheets of pattern paper, pencils, measuring tape, and pincushions planted with needles. A particular pincushion comes to mind. It looked like a Holland tomato; it might have passed for a child's soft toy. Bolts of cloth leaned in corners. The shop's back door opened onto an alley where my mother went to smoke. She smoked inside, too, constantly, and I remember wondering what her customers thought when they carried home clothes that smelled as if they'd been worn to a nightclub. Wherever my mother was in her shop—standing at the worktable in her bare feet, measuring cloth; or rummaging around in the back, sorting through woollens and silks imported from Asia and Europe; or relaxing, legs crossed, in one of the chairs near the front door—her ashtray and her lighter and her coffee cup were close at hand. Also near the entrance were garment racks draped with clothes left by the few clients who had somehow happened on the place, or who knew my mother from AA or from her life before sobriety.

In this cramped and vaguely unsafe environment, my chain-smoking, coughing mother began to realize a fashion aesthetic that was, I believe, arguably original and defiantly antisocial.

The garment I often see, whenever I talk to my dead mother, is a silk kimono. Or it is not a kimono, exactly; it is a robe, hemmed short, that appears kimono-like. The body is white. The sleeves, too, are white, and are encircled with wide bands of machine-made ivory lace. There is a hint of Chanel in the thinner white bands that occur near the seams linking the sleeves to the body, and in the bunched-up lengths of silk crêpe, one in aquamarine, another in a darker blue, and a third in indigo, which are wrapped, in a slightly militaristic style, around each shoulder, and held in place by narrow ribbons sewn like belt loops. These blue and indigo sashes descend from the loops, cascading down the sides of the kimono beneath the arms, and are weighted with horsehair tassels, twelve in all, shaped like angels.

Suspended over each breast of the kimono, from threads attached to detachable shining stars, are two metallic birds like Christmas-tree ornaments. One tethered bird is yellow and in flight; its opposite is pink and at rest. Directly beneath these swinging birds is a green field of fabric in the shape of a valentine heart, half appearing on the kimono's right side, half on the left. If the garment's overall ground is the kimono's white silk, then the ground atop that ground is the divided green heart, which can be made whole by closing the kimono at the front. The heart, which stands about ten inches in height, serves as the locus for a gathering of ostensibly reassuring visual elements. On one side, where, if this were a medical illustration, an atrial chamber might appear, a fuzzy white cat—a cat like the dandruffy white cat my mother then had—sits stitched in place. A giraffe peeks from behind the top of the other side, as if looking curiously over a green hill. The scene is pastoral, a nursery picture. In keeping with the theme of childhood innocence, more green fabric extends down and around the garment's sides in the form of two winding, ever-narrowing pathways bordered with elaborately stitched flowers. I am unable to look at these flowers without remembering the poppy fields in *The Wizard of Oz*.

There is more. Ribbons attached in the neighborhood of the green heart hang down below the robe's bottom hem. At the ends of the ribbons are several found and custom-made objects: a piece of quartz, an empty pillbox, a charm made of metal and beads, a peacock feather, and a small pouch—a coin purse—knitted from brightly colored yarn. There are two lace sachets—of the frilly sort found in farmhouse bedroom dressers—filled with potpourri. Another ornament, made of felt and shaped like a banana, is, in fact, a yellow man in the moon, featuring a pointy nose, a broad mouth, and sleepy eyes.

In order to see the real action taking place on this garment, however, one must carefully turn it over, lay it flat, and study the back.

At the bottom, there is a section of dark-blue and white

overshot—a traditional handwoven fabric used mainly for bed-covers—cut more or less in the shape of a pedestal. Flanking the pedestal are four decorative patches, two on each side, made from floral embroidered silks in black, gold, pink, bronze, silver, white, and blue. The patches are stitched on at angles. Are they meant to look like pockets? Are they badges? There's something purposefully crazy about their off-kilter placement, as if they were intended to communicate the designer's sense of spontaneity and play, her awareness of the life to be found in all things, even remnants of cloth. Directly above the dancing patches runs the continuation of the band of green fabric that began on the garment's front as the flowered pathways branching off from the perimeter of the heart. On the robe's back, this green strip is no longer bordered with flowers; it is hung with bronze and silver pendants—coins, seashells, and starfish. A lion and a horse, made from painted bamboo, descend from strings attached to the kimono's mid-regions; they function to-gether as toy sentinels guarding a complicated piece of Chinese fabric that looks, from a distance, a little like the head depicted in Edvard Munch's *The Scream*. Instead of Munch's wailing face, however, there can be found, at the center of this fabric, a waterbird—a golden crane with a black beak, dark eyes, and a red crest. Around this crane my mother has sewn a standard—a green organza horseshoe, held in place by loops of silver ribbon. The tail ends of the standard are tasseled—not with ornamental angels but with delicate white tassels, the kind appropriate, I would think, for a fringe on a lamp shade.

One more feature needs description. This is an object that covers—as if it had flown in from mountainous lands where gi-ant, benign creatures dwell; found itself over southern Florida;

gazed down and seen, from high above the clouds, my mother at work in her shop; then descended and landed in her fields of silk, where it got comfortable and decided to stay—this object, as I was saying, covers the entire upper back of the kimono. It is an enormous, enormously winged, butterfly.

The body of the butterfly is something my mother bought in a store. Its skin is paper, stretched over a lightweight wooden frame, and brightly painted. I suspect it may be an Indonesian export. It is three-dimensional and elongated—with a proper head, an abdomen, and a waspish tail—and is attached to the garment along the back seam, running head to tail down the wearer's spine. Its outstretched wings, which are made of soft, quilted silk, reach to the kimono's shoulders and are a dull white, painted with pastel swirls and stripes. With its outstretched wings—and as if in imitation of nature's strategy of imitation—the creature looks like a kite. The wings reach to the kimono's shoulders. As a crowning touch, the butterfly displays two delicate antennae that extend upward from its head. In photographs of the robe, these antennae are long and spiraling. Somewhere along the way, however, the antennae have been broken. They're short, splintered.

For more than ten years, my mother had run a program in fashion, textiles, and costume history at Miami–Dade Community College. She had a small faculty under her, and many students. Frequently, she was up and out of the house by sunrise. She might not return before evening. She slept little. Instead, she drank. My father was her partner in this. As evening turned to night, the two of them fought. As the night got late, she went after him with greater and greater fury. A woman had come between my parents in the early years of their marriage, and brought about their first divorce. After their remarriage, when I was nine and my sister, Terry, eight—and until their relationship ended for good—the memory of that woman haunted our family. Many times, following a bout of fighting, when my mother had tumbled into bed or lost consciousness in a chair, my father wept and apologized.

"I'm sorry," he would say to me and my sister, and the look on his face showed that he meant it. But though he did not intend to, and could not have known it, he was apologizing our mother out of existence. He was apologizing himself and his children out of existence, when he whispered to Terry and me, "Your mother works hard all day at school. She works so hard. She's just tired. She's tired."

"She's not tired!" I shouted back. "She's an alcoholic!" No one was listening. Who pays attention to an unhappy fifteen-year-old? And, after all, my mother wasn't the only one who was tired. All our lives were given over to her. I once marveled that my father could endure my mother. I found his martyrdom, as I thought of it then, honorable. It seemed to me that our family was guided by a bleak, incomprehensible fate. It wasn't incomprehensible, though, and it wasn't fate that was guiding us. It was alcohol.

After the nights came the mornings. My sister and I got out of our beds, put on clothes, and marched from the house to the corner where the school bus stopped. In this we took our mother's lead, our mother who lit a morning cigarette, swallowed her coffee, and, without memory of herself in her darker form, went to the office. In those days, the early seventies, her work at the college did not figure much in our family's daily life. It was not something that we talked about. It was never celebrated. She was alone in her work, and she was alone at home, and her isolation—from her family and from the world—informed her use of fashion and design to tell her life story.

But there is a problem. Fashion—and I refer not only to clothes, stylish or otherwise, and the ways they evolve and are worn, but to the meanings and associations that can be drawn from stylistic variations or the lack of variations in clothes—fashion, whether or not considered a high art form, remains explicitly a visual and tactile language, a language, as I have come to understand from reading the work of the art historian Anne Hollander, written in an alphabet of colors, shapes, textures, and forms that subtly shift and change from season to season, and from year to year, over the decades of our lifetimes. Fashion is a communal dialogue, a conversation that never stops—on the subjects of desire, power, kinship, sex, and the passing of time—between people living together in a society. What happens to the conversation, though, when the primary society known by a maker of clothes consists of a dying family—a family which, night after night, year after year, apologizes itself out of existence?

There was a week in the early nineties when my mother, driving her station wagon from Miami, and I, flying south from New York, met in Black Mountain, North Carolina, at the home of her parents. She'd brought with her a selection of her wearable creations, and she was eager to show them off. One night after dinner, she led me and my grandparents to the hallway closet. One by one, she pulled out the garments she'd been working on in her shop near the Miami River, the garments she thought of as works of art. Among them, I recall, was the kimono adorned with butterfly wings.

I watched the faces of her elderly, southern Presbyterian parents. My mother's mother touched the fabrics and said, "Oh, look at this," and "How about that." And she appreciated, in a reserved though generous manner, her daughter's workmanship with needle and thread. But what, exactly, had my mother made with needle and thread? This wasn't clear to me or to my grandparents, who were, frankly, distraught. They didn't know what to say to their daughter.

After a long moment, we retreated from the closet in the hallway. We went to the living room and sat. The television was tuned to the Tony Awards. My mother had always loved Broadway musicals. After a while, I looked away from the screen and saw, on my mother's face and in her slumped posture, in the way she blew cigarette smoke forcibly from her mouth, her angry disappointment.

Had she pulled out hangers draped with clothing that showed either an ironic exaggeration or a direct repudiation of contemporary fashion ideals—glamorously deglamorized dresses in the mid-nineties Comme des Garçons mode, for instance, or radical versions of men's suits executed as statements to be worn by women—her parents might have been similarly perplexed and anxious. But I would have understood that she was making something that, however odd her choices might have appeared at first glance, could nevertheless be worn in the world in a way that communicated to the viewer, in a relatively direct manner, aspects of her desires and her attitudes about the body, about shape and form, about seduction and the politics of public life. I understand that a comparison between my mother's clothes and European and American runway designs is not entirely fair. I also realize that her parents and her son were not the perfect audience for her fantastic productions. She showed us her work. We fled. She risked our misunderstanding and disapprobation, our attempts at praise, our confusion and neglect. In this risk and its result—her suffering—she found proof of herself as an original and subversive artist.

Was it so? Was my mother ahead of her time, destined for acceptance by some future civilization, as she proclaimed more than once in the years leading up to her death?

The robe is titled "The Heroine's Journey," and yet it is neutral in relation to the wearer's sexuality. It does not shape itself around the body, and it does not impose shape on the body. From a distance, it looks like a vestment worn by an Episcopal priest; though, with its tassels and wings, it is clearly more pagan than Protestant. It is a peaceable kingdom crowded with personal spirit guides and pets—birds, lion, horse, giraffe, cat—a menagerie of wild and tame hieroglyphs guiding the kimono's wearer, the heroine, safely down the green road bordered with flowers and paved with magical coins. The robe takes on the life of all the lives emblazoned on or suspended from it, and it imparts this life to the person wearing it. But what manner of life is it? Neither earthbound nor confined within the mortal body, it is a life that is at once sacred and secular, shapeless and formal, youthful and aged, innocent and experienced, ancient and modern, fleeting and everlasting.

The year before she died, I met my mother in Philadelphia. It was the spring of 1999. Her father had been dead for four years, and her mother was soon to follow. Not long after her father's passing, my mother had abandoned Miami and her air-conditioned shop beneath the expressway overpasses. She'd packed up her sewing machines, her tailor's dummies, her buttons, her worktable, her fabrics and scissors, her pincushions and measuring tapes, and Merlin, her new cat—the white one had finally given up the ghost—and, using money left by my grandfather, she'd purchased a little one-story house at the bottom of a road in Black Mountain. Now, three years later, she'd driven north to attend the art school graduation of F., a friend from the Florida years who had left Miami to study painting in Philadelphia. At the ceremony, F. and my mother met a gallery owner who worked in the Old City district. This person expressed interest in my mother's clothes, and my mother formed the impression that the gallery would give her a show.

One Saturday morning in May, I got on a train to Philadelphia. F. lived in a red brick house on a quiet Center City street. I took my time walking from the station. I had a bad feeling about the day ahead. My mother's health had been rapidly declining in recent years, and in the past months she'd sounded, when I'd spoken with her on the phone, sicker and sicker. I was afraid of what I was going to see.

I wasn't wrong to worry. When I saw my mother, I wanted nothing more than to lower my head, turn away, and walk steadily and without stopping back to the station.

Instead, she and F. and I went out to a café. I did my best to suppress my embarrassment at my mother's loud speaking voice. It seemed to me that she was trumpeting and boasting. Were people staring? I recall that F. was wearing a jacket my mother had made, a short coat decorated with contrasting fabric pieces stitched in geometric patterns. F. wore the garment comfortably. If the embellished kimono represented couture, the jacket might have come from the Peace Goods sportswear line. I wondered, as I sat with my coffee, whether F. would continue wearing it once my mother got in her car and headed south.

We paid the check, got up from the table, and began our pilgrimage to the gallery where my mother hoped to be welcomed as a new artist. It was a long journey over a short distance. I watched my mother struggling to breathe; and I noticed her preparing to reach for the nearest fixed object, a lamppost or a parking meter that could steady her, if she suddenly needed it. Had she gained weight? Lost weight? What about the cough? Had her hacking grown worse? Why did her hair look so dead? Was she having trouble carrying her portfolio? And where had she got to all of a sudden?

"Mom? Mom?"

There she was, half a block behind, standing in the heat, lighting a cigarette with a shaking hand, looking lost.

"Mom, are you all right? Do you want to rest a minute?"

"No. I'm fine. I don't need to rest. Let's get to the gallery. How far is it, Don?"

"It's not far. It's up here. Can you make it? Do you want me to carry your portfolio?"

"No."

"Have you seen a doctor, Mom?"

"I have a doctor at home, Don. Let's get to the gallery. They're expecting me. I have an appointment."

But what kind of appointment? When we finally got down the block and through the door, the woman behind the front desk recommended that my mother leave slides and a résumé and wait to be contacted. This is normal-enough procedure, but my mother, who had garrulously promoted the narrative of her imminent ascension, took it as a blow. She stood before the receptionist's desk. I was terrified that she would make a scene. I felt her anger and her humiliation, and my own humiliation. I paced around the gallery space, then sneaked out and paced some more, back and forth, on the sidewalk. It was a while before my mother and F. came outside. F. encouraged my mother not to get upset. But my mother had tipped into one of her bitter, bewildered moods.

The walk to F.'s house was only a few blocks. Nevertheless, it was too much to ask of my mother, so we hailed a taxi. When we got to F.'s, we decided to have an early supper. There was leftover fried chicken in the refrigerator, and we could eat outside. F.'s street was a dead end and got little traffic; the residents used the street and the sidewalk as a kind of communal square, and they occasionally set up chairs and tables beneath the old trees that formed a low canopy overhead.

It was evening, and the air was warm and still. The three of us sat in a circle, eating with our hands. For years, my mother had had the habit, in public and in private, of announcing, as an artist, her identification with me. She believed that we understood each other, and were fundamentally alike in our alienation from the noncreative world. "We don't need to worry about what other people think, Don," she might say. And she might add, "We don't fit in."

My mother may have made a few such claims that night when she, F., and I sat down to dinner. I don't remember. All I could do was watch her eat.

She sat facing me. She took large bites, and bits of food

spilled down her front as she chewed. She ate, it seemed to me, without awareness of herself; and the impression she gave was of something gone wrong, as if perhaps, at age sixty-four, she were making her first attempt to learn table skills. She wasn't a toddler, though; she was sick, and denying her sickness. In four months, she would learn that she was dying.

I looked away. I was a man in his forties, afraid of his mother. Or maybe I was afraid for her. I looked again, and we made eye contact, and it crossed my mind that she was a crazy person wearing crazy clothes of her own crazy design, with a crazy person's hairdo atop a head brimming with strange hallucinations in which she conversed with a crew of spirits that included the Virgin Mary and Jesus himself. These spirits related to her as a peer. The fact of their communications reinforced her belief in herself as spiritually and emotionally superevolved, and this belief, in turn, supported her image of herself as a heroine on a journey. In this romantic-journey scenario, her failures and losses in life were grand successes, insofar as they represented trials too arduous for anyone but a hero to overcome.

In spirit, the kimono reflects its maker's predicament. My mother's entire relationship to fashion was one of passionate ambivalence. Her mother had pushed her into vocational home economics in both high school and college, and she later envied my father, a teacher of literature, his exalted access to higher things. She never wore the French and Italian designs that she showed her students in pictures during those years when she had an academic job. She liked to drive to the Neiman Marcus store in Bal Harbour, but she rarely, if ever, bought anything. She said that she could not afford Chanel and

Dior, but I suspect that the truth was more complex. The coats and hats and dresses she most admired represented for her, I think, a world beyond her compass. In the sixties, when she and my father were beginning their first divorce, she led a group of fashion students on a European tour, and later she took a few trips overseas and to New York, but these places remained faraway lands. In the seventies, after remarrying my father, she got her Ph.D. from the College of Home Economics at Florida State University—her dissertation was titled "Exploratory Study of Quality Control Problems and Procedures in the Manufacture of Junior and Misses Fashion Apparel in Dade County, Florida"—but she never felt that this achievement was appreciated by her family or her colleagues. It would be only a short time before she'd turn her back on teaching. In the late eighties and the nineties, her Peace Goods years, she began exploring popular alternative philosophies, most of which were formed, it seemed to me, from blends of astrology, Jungian psychology, Native American mythology, and various recovered-memory and past-life regression theories and therapies—the ad hoc religions of the New Age. These philosophies essentially gave my mother permission to imagine the world as a place of her own making. She never, I sometimes think, stopped being a child.

The world depicted on the kimono is the world inhabited by that child, a world full of storybook animals waiting to accompany the heroine on her journey to forever. To see her wearing it, however—and I recall that I did, one day at her house in North Carolina, though I wonder, sometimes, whether I only imagined this—was to experience its power. My mother was tall and sedentary, and in her later years she ate poorly. Drinking and smoking had broken her down. Her face looked worn and, as my father had always said, tired. That day in Black Mountain, she put on the robe, drew it close around her, and stooped beneath the low ceiling in her living room, the room partly taken up with the worktable she'd carted north from her shop in Miami.

The kimono fell on my mother to a place between her hips and knees. The butterfly's antennae rose in the air behind her head, and drew attention to her hair, which looked brushed to appear as if it had not been brushed at all, then hurriedly sprayed in place. She had on glasses; their frames were big and buglike; combined with the antennae and the wings, the effect was almost comical. Because I knew that I had no choice other than to approve, I told her that the kimono was amazing, and she asked me if I truly thought so, and I said, "Yes, yes, absolutely."

I imagine her turning, showing me the back, like a lover displaying a dress that delivers a frank promise of sex. And it occurs to me that the butterfly was a parasite—that its wings were too small to lift and carry both her and all the things attached to the robe, the sachets and the man in the moon and the feathers and jewels hanging from ribbons and strings. When I see her this way, in memory, with the indigo and blue sashes dangling beneath her arms, and the cat like a badge over her heart, and her antennae sticking up behind her head, I become grateful to her father, who, however he may have failed her when she was a little girl, protected her and insured her a home in the last years of her life.

In the seventies, my mother made a suit for my father. We were living in Coconut Grove at the time, in a house that had formerly been inhabited by a CIA agent. The suit was hand-made in the traditional manner, with recurrent fittings leading to the drawing and redrawing of patterns, and the painstaking construction of a paper-and-muslin facsimile. In proper tailoring, enormous labor is expended before the valuable fabric—in this case, a dark-brown wool herringbone from a Scottish mill—is ever cut. The tailor observes the posture, mannerisms, and physical idiosyncrasies of the man who will wear the finished garment. Subtle information about social standing, power, and ambition is communicated through the wearer's bearing, and through choices in material and style: pinstripes or plaids; notched lapels or peaked; side vents or center; and so on. The tailor indeed takes the measure of the man, who begins to feel the pride that comes with wearing clothes cut and sewn specifically for his body, clothes intended to carry him into the world as a confident and vital participant in society.

The suit my mother made for my father was impeccable. He told me that he wore it until he wore it out. My mother's skill as a tailor is evident in all the clothes she ever made. Yet when it comes to the apparel she championed as wearable works of art—and tried without success to market as her Peace Goods line—there remains the problem of power. The power of my mother's robe is the power that was strongest in her at the end of her life. This was her power to force away the people she loved. There is beauty in the robe, as there was beauty in my mother, who, when young, was lively and playful and striking to look at, and who even in her worst sickness never lost her ability to laugh. But it is likely, for a person newly confronted with her kimono, that the naked innocence it reveals will defy empathy. When this happens, the conversation among the maker, the wearer, and the viewer of clothes, the conversation open to all of us, simply through living in a world where people get dressed, will be interrupted.

That my mother knew so thoroughly her craft and the traditions of fashion, and that she went on to make, in her final decade, such declamatory yet incomprehensible clothes, such odd things to wear, gives—in light of her scornful retreat from people and the public world—a supreme, unexpected dignity to her creations. I realize now, as I did not before she died, that, however violent or delusional she may have been when I was growing up, she was, after all, working. She was smoking and drinking herself into her grave, yet she was managing, in her classrooms at the college, and in her shop near the river, and in her house at the bottom of the road, to carry on and endure. "Death? Or life?" the kimono seems to ask. Because the appliquéd symbols that form these questions are so appropriate to the idea of ceremony and pageantry, and yet so childlike and puzzling, the viewer looks away from the garment and considers the wearer. But my mother in her robe is nowhere to be found. Her inner life has been transferred to the surface of the kimono.

My mother lived her life inviting death. When her cancer was diagnosed, and she was summarily ordered by her doctors to quit smoking, she did so in a matter of days, and seemed afterward rarely to think of smoking, or to regret that she ever had. Smoking had got her to the one place where the major competing strains in her consciousness of herself—as a visionary child and as a brokenhearted woman—came together, and made her whole, and left her to die in peace.

Years after her death, my worry over her persists. Worry

may be what I am trying to overcome when I talk to my dead mother, as I did that evening in the stairwell at the New York Public Library. I was brooding over some problem that had existed between us, and sharing with her, out loud (though not too loudly), my thoughts. On the first-floor landing, I briefly imagined her floating near the ceiling. Stitched onto her silk kimono were provisions and companions for her winged journey into eternity. "Mom!" I said, and, as I called out to her, I did not glance over my shoulder, and I did not, in that passing instant, dare to see, at a modest height above the ground—my mother, not there.

PART V

have often wondered what might have happened to my mother after she finally stopped drinking, in 1983, had it not been for her father, who, I suspect, worried over his daughter every day of his life as a parent, and who, in the years leading up to his death at the age of ninety, energetically sought reassurance, typically from me, though also from my sister, that his daughter would one day overcome her anger and make a place for herself in the world.

"Don, what do you think of your mother's prospects?" he would ask me whenever I visited him and my grandmother in North Carolina. "Do you think she's doing all right?"

All right? I never knew quite what to say. Should I speak the truth and risk upsetting him? Sometimes I said nothing. I remember sitting on the sofa in the house on McCoy Cove Road, feeling helpless, looking out the living-room window at the low gray mountains nearby.

My grandparents' house was neither beautiful nor remarkable—not like many Black Mountain residences, some of which had been built as vacation bungalows in the Arts and Crafts style—but it was a good house, and my grandparents, while in their seventies and eighties, had done painstaking work on it and on the narrow, sloping yard that was given over, out back, to shade trees overhanging a picnic table, and to my grandfather's vegetable garden and my grandmother's flower beds. There was a garage out back, too, at the end of the driveway that passed the house as it climbed the grade from the road. Sometimes when he was in a storytelling mood, my grandfather might slip away through the kitchen and across the patio and up the driveway to his workroom at the back of the garage. A moment later, steady on his feet, and chewing a toothpick or a stick of Dentyne, he would come inside the house, lower himself into his chair, and begin volubly speaking. Often, my grandmother got up and left the room, because she did not approve of his drinking.

My favorites of his stories took place in the mountains. My grandparents had graduated—she in 1926, he a year later—from Tusculum College in Greenville, Tennessee. At around the time they were there, I remember him telling me, a scholarship was endowed by a widow who lived in, of all places, Miami, Florida. It was the widow's desire, as I recall my grandfather's understanding of things, that part of her money be used to educate students from the poorer reaches of the western Appalachias. She had herself been a child of the mountains, I remember from the story, and, through education, had found her way into the modern world. Because the pupils brought to Tusculum under her scholarship were largely unschooled, the college committed itself to their comprehensive education. In return, the matriculated men and women—who might go on to train in medicine or law or engineering, but who, I gathered, often quit with teaching degrees—promised to return to their home communities, where they would live and work for a set term of years.

Neither of my grandparents was a recipient of the scholarship. But for a time after he graduated, my grandfather recruited for it. He told of driving a Model A Ford along dirt trails and over hilltops and through narrow mountain hollows; sometimes, he said, he drove up creek beds. When he came across a house or a small subsistence farm, he would get out of the car and ask whether the inhabitants knew of any young people who might want to go to college. Were there any around, he would ask, who showed signs of being school material?

One of my grandfather's tales had him driving a rocky creek bed that led toward a mountain hamlet. As my grandfather neared the hamlet, he heard rifle fire echoing from the darkness behind the trees. When he got close enough to see buildings, the firing let up. My grandfather drove into a clearing surrounded with old structures that featured cluttered porches on which, I seem to recall him saying, dogs and children sat eyeing him. It was a poor place, like most all the places he visited in that job, a place that I picture as a scene in a photograph taken by Walker Evans or one of the other photographers who worked for the Works Progress Administration during the Depression. That day, men with guns pointed toward the ground came out into the open—they came from here and there, not in a group—and gathered in a circle around my grandfather's car, where they politely discussed his business with him. When that was done, my grandfather got back in his Model A and drove on. I can imagine one of the men saying to him, "Go on up that way and you'll find a boy," then waving a hand in the air. The mountain men retreated into the forest from which they'd come, and, after my grandfather had got a short distance away, their firing resumed. It is not clear to me whether my grandfather knew with certainty, or believed with conviction, that the men had been taking aim at each other. But I remember that he sometimes talked about the feud between the Hatfields and the McCoys, which took place in the West Virginia and Kentucky mountains not terribly far north of the Tennessee farm country where he and my grandmother had been raised. The Hatfield-McCoy feud involved deliberate assassinations and a love affair, though it did not, contrary to folklore, carry on for scores of years. It lasted from 1878 until 1890, and exerted a tremendous hold on the imaginations of people living in that part of the world in the years during and immediately after its heyday as news.

According to my grandfather, one of the students who came to Tusculum under the widow's scholarship had been born into a feud. O., a Kentucky boy, arrived at the college wearing a sidearm beneath his coat. O.'s father had killed a man and gone into hiding—not so much from the law as from the victim's kin—and O. had vowed, in the event his father was killed by the man's relatives, to avenge the death. For this reason, O.'s revolver never left his side. Did O. carry the gun to class? I might ask my grandfather, interrupting the narrative. Did he hide it in his pants at a Saturday-night dance? Did he keep it loaded beside the books on his desk? My grandfather thought he might have done these things. O. was ready at a moment's notice to abandon school and hunt for revenge.

Until that time, he studied literature. It was customary in those days, the story went, for Tusculum students to produce a play at commencement, and in his senior year O. was encouraged by his teachers to write the play. My grandfather claimed to have seen the production, and described the work as a loving portrayal of O.'s family, and as an unromantic though somewhat comical depiction of backwoods poverty, stern religion, and alcoholism. It was, I suppose—and if I correctly understood my grandfather's remarks about it—a work of American naturalism, possibly an accidental work of naturalism, and, I suspect, in keeping with styles taking hold on the American stage during the years between the world wars. This style could be seen in the works of Eugene O'Neill and others who had studied under George Pierce Baker, whose drama seminars at Harvard placed the literature of the theater in an active and responsive rather than a purely academic and literary context. Great plays are authentic, living stories of a civilization, and, in Baker's view, the plays then being written for the American stage required, in order that our society could find itself mirrored in its contemporary theater, a milieu in which practical training in professional stagecraft might bring into existence a class of artists able to conceive and perfect what amounted to a new American art form. Baker's famous classes became a foundation for the Yale School of Drama, founded in 1925. According to my grandfather, the commencement speaker for O.'s graduating class at Tusculum was a colleague of Baker's who had gone to teach at the Drama School in New Haven. At the performance of O.'s play, which received rousing applause when the curtain came down, this guest speaker, startled to his feet by O.'s unexpected talent, promised him, before God and the Tusculum community, a place at Yale.

"What happened?" I sometimes asked my grandfather at this point in the story. It was our call and response.

He chewed his toothpick. "If I have it right, he went up to New Haven, and was there a year or two. I believe he might even have had a play produced in New York."

"Did he carry his pistol?"

"Yes, he must have. He wanted to be ready to get up and go if he needed. He didn't want to stop and so much as pack his bags. He wanted to catch the first train home. Well, one day he got word that his father had been shot. It was what he'd been waiting for. He folded the telegram and put it in his pocket and walked to the station and was never seen at Yale again."

"He went to the mountains."

"Yes. For years he tracked his father's killer, but he never found the man."

"Never."

"Some years ago I was in Kentucky, Don, and I looked him up. He told me that after leaving Yale he dedicated himself to finding the killer. But eventually he realized that he simply would not find him. There was too much territory to cover. Don, you can walk twenty feet into those woods and lose your sense of direction and never come out. So he gave up. He became a teacher. By the time I found him, he was long retired."

"Did he keep writing?"

"That's a good question. I don't know. I don't believe he did, Don. I don't think he did. Too much time had passed."

But getting to the story at hand:

In 1994, my grandparents, too old to maintain their house, moved into a nearby assisted-living community, where they occupied a small apartment with a tiny yard planted with flowers. Several times I visited them there—an insomniac man in his mid-thirties, walking the long corridors of a rural home for the aged. I remember from those trips that the men and women of the place, who seemed ancient to me when I first arrived, began, as the days passed, to appear younger and more beautiful. The women in particular, in their laughter and their smiles, and in the way they might quickly glance away when aware of being looked at, showed evidence of themselves in their youth. I felt charmed by the ladies in my grandparents' circle, and learned to understand that a woman near the end of her life has not given up her powers of seduction. While stopping after lunch to say hello, I might look into the eyes of a great-grandmother from Richmond or Atlanta and see, or imagine seeing, the girl who did not yet realize that everything and everyone ahead of her—the husband who would pass away, her children, and their children, since moved to distant cities— could come and go so quickly.

One afternoon in 1995, while I was talking to my grandfather about things that had happened before I was born, I saw a startled look pass across his face, as if he had seen something unexpected, and, in that instant, I was sure he'd felt the speed of time. A month later, on an October night, he walked into the bathroom, had a heart attack, and fell to the floor. He was ninety. Four years later, in the late summer of 1999, my grandmother followed him in her sleep. And two weeks after that, my mother, who had moved to North Carolina in the year following her father's death, collapsed and was taken in an ambulance to an Asheville hospital.

It was not a surprise. At her mother's funeral, her face looked worn and gray, the color of damp ash, and she was feverish and trembling. She could barely stand. When had my mother become such an old woman? Her cough had grown nightmarish, frightening to listen to. At her mother's service, listening to her, it was possible to feel the worry and discomfort of the people sitting in the pews behind us, our grandmother's elderly friends from church and town, and the small handful of relatives who'd driven in a single car across the mountains from eastern Tennessee, my mother's uncle Orbin and her cousin Annette and aunt Dorothy. After the service, my mother found her way outside the church, where her cough abated long enough for her to light a cigarette and send herself into another fit.

That night, my sister and I stood on the porch at our hotel, and I told her that I thought our mother was a dangerous person. I said that I did not want to be alone with our mother. I said that I did not think our mother would live much longer. "A year? Two years?" I guessed. Then I suggested that Terry and I get ready for bad news ahead, because when the time came it would be up to us alone to handle our dying mom, who, during much of our childhoods, had been a drunk, a woman we had known—and, I think, in our memories, in our consciousnesses of ourselves, and in our bodies, continue to know—as a holy terror.

I remember my phone conversation with my mother, just over a week after my grandmother's funeral. It was the morning after she'd been rushed to the Asheville hospital. I was back in Brooklyn. I sat perched on a low ottoman—slumped over, as if hiding in my own house. I pressed the telephone receiver against my ear, and my mother whispered that she was ready to die, and that she knew peace awaited her in the Universe. She told me she loved me, and would continue loving me when she was dead.

After hearing that, I had a conversation with her pulmonary specialist, who told me that my mother would not recover, and that invasive or aggressive therapies were out of the question. Radiation might give her ten months to a year. If the malignancy were left to grow unchecked, infections brought about through the blockage of one lung would kill her in half that time.

"Your mother has made it clear that she intends to refuse the radiation," he told me.

We talked a while longer. He asked me about my own smoking, and I admitted to some; he suggested that it would be better not to do it, and I agreed. I thanked him and hung up the phone, then made my way out of the living room and down the hall, passing the dimly lit bathroom and the little extra room that, before too long, would be packed and spilling over with uncrated marble-top bureaus, rolled and folded-over rugs, and carefully wrapped and boxed smaller items saved from my grandparents' house out on McCoy Cove Road, and, from my mother's house, old artworks and an Art Nouveau lamp and a stained-glass vase and an ivory brooch—all the various belongings that I could not part with, yet which I fear I will never learn to live with. I made my way down the hall, as I was saying, to the bedroom, where R., my girlfriend at that time, waited under the sheets. I got in bed beside her, and, after I'd cried a long time, she and I made love, and, at some point in the day, I got out of bed and phoned the airlines and packed a suitcase, and, early the next morning, I was off.

My first stop was the Charlotte airport. I called my father in Miami from a pay phone in the commuter-flight terminal. I told him how things were, and he told me how sorry he was, and then we were silent. I remember waiting for him to say something more. Or was my father waiting for me? He and my mother had, after all, been high school sweethearts. Not long ago, while sorting through a box of family photographs, I found a picture cut from a Sarasota newspaper.

"Panhellenic members lived it up this week, when they had a holiday dance at Tropicana," the caption begins. My future parents, home on vacation from college, sit across a table from another couple. It's the mid-fifties, and my mother has on black evening gloves; her hands rest on a table draped with a plain white tablecloth. She wears a sleeveless, backless white dress fastened at the throat with a choker made from darker fabric—it appears in the picture, though it is impossible to tell, for sure, that the choker closes with a brooch. Her hair is pulled out of the way in a hairdo that is difficult to see in detail. She wears costume pearl earrings of a sort that I remember her putting on for parties when I was a boy. Smiling, she gazes down and away from her future husband, who, sitting beside her—from the camera's point of view, my father is more or less behind her—and wearing a dark jacket, a narrow, tightly knotted tie, and a white pocket square, leans in close with one elbow propped on the table. His open hand rests near her bare arm. But he does not appear to be touching her. Instead, he is staring at her face in profile. Frankly, uninhibitedly, he appraises her. And my mother-to-be, aware of his eyes on her, aware of being *seen* by him (and by the camera)—is an alluringly beautiful, coy young woman. Unless I am mistaken, she is in love.

That day on the telephone in the Charlotte airport, I listened as my father described Hurricane Floyd, at that moment racing toward Miami. Floyd was expected to make landfall with greater force than 1992's Andrew, which had ripped apart entire districts of the city. My father was preparing his house for Floyd. He and his wife had, at that time, two old, sick cats. My father doted on the cats. He told me that he and my stepmother planned to wait out the storm with their pets in a barricaded bedroom closet.

"What?"

My father and his wife were professors at a Miami university. Surely the campus would offer better protection than their house. True, my father told me. Unfortunately, the shelters would not admit animals. I thought about what he was telling me, and then shouted, "Dad, if you want to use your body to shield your cats from a force-five hurricane, I can't help you! My mother is dying! She's *dying!*"

I slammed down the phone, showed my boarding pass at the gate, and marched onto the plane to Asheville. I was breathing heavily, and perspiring. My father's love for his animals had undone me—and what had I done but angrily show my own powerlessness?

One way that I have for years maintained a relative powerlessness is by neglecting to keep a valid driver's license. I let my Florida license, the one I'd had throughout college, expire after several years in New York, and learned to rely on public and commercial transportation, like a European. My sister would be joining me in two days; she could rent a car. During the flight, I stared from the airplane window at the Smokies below. It was a clear, hot day in September. The plane, bouncing on wind currents, was headed into the sun. After landing, all alone with the driver in an enormous van I'd hired to take me from the airport to the hospital, I watched the day's light fading behind a western ridge of the same green mountains I'd seen from the air.

At Mission–St. Joseph's Hospital, it took me a while to find my mother's room. I lost my sense of direction and rode up and down in elevators. The old people I came across in the halls looked neither beautiful nor youthful. Quite a few were gasping for air in the rooms on the hall that led to my mother's, which, thanks to her lung infection, was stickered with brightly colored quarantine notices.

I knocked lightly, opened the door, and peeked in. She was propped up in bed. "Mom?"

"Don?"

I put down my suitcase, walked across the room, leaned over, and, cautious of the tubes and hoses connecting her to pieces of equipment, hugged her.

"How're you feeling?"

"Not great."

"I'm sorry."

"You don't have to be sorry, Don. Was your trip all right? I'm glad you're here. Thank you for coming," she said. After that we made an effort, for a while, to talk as if nothing out of the ordinary were taking place—the way people in crises will, I suppose—and suddenly she asked, "Don, are you going to dedicate your next book to me?"

My first had been dedicated to her parents, the second to my father and his brother, my uncle Eldridge, who'd died in 1992. The third, about some misbehaving psychoanalysts in a nameless city, was scheduled to appear in early 2000.

I was trapped. Obviously, she was next in line. But I didn't particularly want to dedicate—certainly not on demand, as it seemed to me in that moment—a book to my mother. I stood in her hospital room and said:

"Well . . ."

"No?"

"What I mean to say is that the new book isn't—it isn't appropriate for dedicating. I've decided not to dedicate it."

What?

"Oh. Will you dedicate one to me sometime?"

"Of course," I promised, and, desperately, went on, "It has to be the right book. Do you know what I mean? Mom?"

"I don't. I don't know, Don. I'm going to die."

"Oh, Mom."

A nurse entered the room and tried to talk to my mother about home care. My mother thought this pointless, because she had determined on her own that the cancer had spread to her brain. She hoped to move directly from the hospital to one of the Hospice facilities known as Solace houses, meant for people in the last stages of illness. I remember that my mother's silver-haired GP stopped by on his evening rounds, but stayed only briefly. I'd booked a night at Asheville's most expensive hotel, far on the other side of town. I had thought that I might, in some unaffordable place far removed from the circumstances defining reality, feel—what? Protected? I told my mother that I'd see her early the next day, called a taxi (which took a long time coming), and, when I arrived at the resort, found the dining rooms closed. I trekked past empty ballrooms and conference halls, and, after several wrong turns, located my room, where I stayed awake until dawn picking at room-service food, watching television, and wishing that I could open the sealed-shut windows.

The windows faced a construction project. The hotel was building a new wing. All of a sudden, the sun was up and the day's work with heavy equipment had begun. I got out of bed and drank coffee, cup after cup. I'd arranged to meet a lawyer my mother had retained for a lawsuit she'd brought against the previous owner of her house, the real estate agent who'd handled the sale, and a Black Mountain oil-company owner. Shortly after moving in, in 1997, she'd smelled fumes. The heating-oil tank in her basement had been leaking into the topsoil. Without a clean bill of health from the EPA, her house—paid for in cash—would be worthless. A suit for damages had dragged on for more than a year, and my mother had made enemies in Black Mountain. I ran downstairs to meet the lawyer, already behind in his day's schedule. He offered to take me to the hospital, and talk along the way. Driving through Asheville, he told me not to worry about the oil underneath the house. He told me that he admired my mother, whom he saw as a courageous person. He asked me if I'd ever married.

"I haven't."

"No? Why not? You ought to try it," he said, and went on to describe his happiness in his second marriage, which had gathered the children from his and his wife's first marriages together in one family.

At the hospital, my mother complained that her GP had not visited that day. One of the nurses thought he might be in the emergency room. I went downstairs and entered the maze of corridors leading to the ER. When I got there, I saw, through the doors to the ward, my mother's doctor. I pushed open the swinging doors, marched past nurses, and asked him if I might speak with him. He put down his clipboard and we chatted—as if getting to know each other—and he told me, "There's nothing we can do about your mother's cancer in the long run, but we can give her time, and she needn't suffer."

"I understand."

"Talk to her about radiation. She's a good lady."

"I'll do what I can," I promised. On my way to see her, though, I had the thought that I might prefer her gone sooner rather than later. When my grandmother died, my mother had proclaimed that, unburdened of lifelong parental constraints, she would be free at last to move to the San Juan Islands, a place she'd never visited, but which she understood to be a secret garden for women artists. Now I was having my own fantasy about the freedom to pursue happiness. All I had to do, I thought, was respect her rejection of medical interventions, and she would die by Christmas from fevers that would make her delirious.

When I got to her room, though, I told her that her doctors were not conspiring to harm her. "They're doctors, Mom. They took an oath." And I begged, "Try radiation?"

"I'll think about it."

"Will you? Please?"

"I said I'd think about it."

A Hospice worker appeared, and my mother said, "It's in my brain! I feel the cancer in my brain!"

The woman said, "You can't usually feel it like that," and turned to me and said that someone would need to be at my mother's house the next morning. A hospital bed, an air compressor and hoses, and portable tanks were scheduled for early delivery.

I could get a lift to Black Mountain, it turned out, from a friend of my mother's who worked near the hospital.

"I have to go get things ready, Mom. They're kicking you out of here in a few days."

She squeezed my hand, laughed, and coughed. "Go ahead, Don."

On the drive, my mother's friend told me about her grown son, whom she had not seen for many years because he refused to visit her. I nodded my head sympathetically and stared out the window at the kudzu strangling the life out of trees and plants beside the highway.

"I don't know whether your mother has told you her theories about your family. I guess she hasn't," the friend said.

"What does she believe?"

"Your mother thinks her father wasn't her father. There was another man in your grandmother's life."

"Jesus."

"Why would your mother *say* that?"

"I don't know. What do you guess? As her friend."

"We're not close anymore," the friend said, and commented on my mother's flair for working people against each other. "It's hard to be close to someone who gets people mad at each other."

We were nearing the Monte Vista Hotel, on Main Street. I had to check in, watch the television for reports on Hurricane Floyd, call R. in New York and rant into the telephone, try later to sleep, wake up at a reasonable hour, and meet the oxygen truck at my mother's house a few blocks away. If time remained before my sister arrived, I might, in the early afternoon, visit the estate lawyer (who was not, I should say, the lawyer working on the oil-spill suit) handling my grandmother's—and, soon, my mother's—last will and testament. In the event, I did what I needed to do (including standing on the Monte Vista lawn sometime after midnight, praying to my grandfather's spirit for any kind of guidance he—it?—could give), and, at the lawyer's office, in a brick house on a quiet street, I was handed a pair of sweetheart wills signed by my grandfather and grandmother in the early eighties, the second of which—my grandmother's, already in probate—left all their worldly goods to my mother.

My grandfather did not leave behind great wealth. Like many in his generation, he had been distrustful of the stock market. Yet he'd been frugal, and had saved enough to help his family when needs arose. Before he died, he told us his intention to draw up a will that would disperse whatever remained, after his and my grandmother's deaths, among my sister, me, and our mother. He told us he wanted to do this out of consideration that his grandchildren were now, like his daughter, adults.

"That's not the will. That's not the will," I said over and over to the confused lawyer.

And later that day, when my sister arrived in the car she'd rented at the Charlotte, North Carolina, airport, I said, practically as she was opening the car door and stepping out, "Mom fucked us."

"What?"

"She took in a 1983 will! She grabbed an old will out of the file! Leaving everything to *her*!"

We set up a labor routine that followed old-fashioned gender lines. My sister occupied our mother's house, phoning nursing agencies and scheduling interviews. I commandeered the hotel bar as a base from which to contact doctors, lawyers, and the woman in charge of the money-market accounts. I saw my mother as a suicide and a cheat who would steal her children's birthright, and I hated her, with her brain-cancer dreams and her banishment of her father, without whom she must have felt orphaned and alone, as did I—a fact that I savagely demonstrated the evening my sister and I drove west on Interstate 40 to the hospital, where we packed our mother's suitcase, put her shoes on her feet, and rolled her in her wheelchair past the nurses' station, into and out of the elevator, across the hospital's expansive lobby, and into the Appalachian night.

We helped her into the rental car's front passenger seat. I recall that I tilted back the seat for her comfort. I loaded the oxygen and her suitcase into the back, then climbed into the car. I was sitting, as I remember, behind my mother, and could see, passing through the space separating the front seats, the clear tubing connecting her nostrils to the squat green tank propped beside me like some strange new addition to the family.

"How are you doing, Mom?" my sister and I asked. "How are you feeling?"

"Okay, kids."

Terry started the car. We began the drive. I couldn't resist. Addressing the back of my mother's head, I said, "Mom, do you remember what Granddaddy told us about his will? Right before he died?"

"What are you *asking* me? I just got out of the *hospital*! I'm sick, Don! I'm *sick*! Can't you let me have some *peace*?"

"Don! Stop!" This from my sister.

I leaned back in my seat. I'd made our mother cry. We rode

home to the sounds of her sobbing and coughing. Later, at the house, she got in her bed and announced that she wanted Terry to keep her company for the night. I had to go to the hotel.

The next day and the day after that, I manned the hotel bar phone. No one I spoke with had heard of another will. I opened the yellow pages and read the names of Asheville attorneys. I was determined to catch my mother in what I was certain was a deliberate deceit. How could she? How *dare* she? I told myself that I wanted to get to the bottom of the matter. I was curious. That was all. Had there been another will? Where was it? Had my grandfather mentioned another lawyer?

Hurricane Floyd had by this time changed course and spun away from the Florida coast. The danger to my father and his wife had passed. At least there was that. But what about the toxic spill beneath my mother's house? What about the Environmental Protection Agency? What about radiation therapy? Would my mother accept radiation? Would she consider a nursing home? Which nursing home?

In the afternoons, I cleared my papers from the bar and walked down the hill to the house. Had you been a resident of one of the homes in that part of town—one of the stone bungalows whose porches, in my memory of them, were painted durable green or brown shades that echoed the colors of the forested mountains in the near distance; or one of the bigger houses whose more spacious porches were decorated with comfortable chairs positioned to give a view of the lawn—and had you been sitting out front or standing at a window, you might have seen a man stalking past, wearing lace-up moccasins without socks, khaki shorts held up by a narrow belt, and a white dress shirt, tucked in. He probably would have had his hands shoved into his pockets, and his head might have been lowered, eyes glaring at the road ahead. Would you have imagined that this anxious man was plotting to bring down shame and maybe even the law on his own mother, who, at that moment, was lying on her back in huge discomfort, possibly imagining dying, or imagining smoking and drinking, or trying, with help from her pills, to lose consciousness and sleep for an hour or two, while in the kitchen her daughter made a few last phone calls of her own, penciled check marks beside things-to-do notes on a yellow pad, and boiled water for tea?

"You look like your father," my mother said to me one afternoon when I came in the house. She was correct. The shorts-and-shirt outfit I was wearing was pretty much a copy of his summer uniform.

It had been a long time since my father had left my mother for good, and for years I'd listened to her criticisms of him. Yet I recall that once, when she was just beginning her new life in North Carolina (before death began waiting, as it were, around the corner), I asked her to tell me about the time when they'd first separated, and she surprised me. I know that her discovery of his love affair, early in their marriage, must certainly have wrecked some part of her confidence in herself as a sexually compelling woman, a confidence that she never, I think, regained, and that her drinking, by incrementally destroying her body and undermining her feelings of well-being and clarity of mind, helped to obliterate further.

And yet in spite of what I know, or think I know, today, it is also true that my memories of my parents' early bad times are obscure to me. I see, for instance, an edge of olive-green carpet on a wood floor, and blue-spined paperback books, old Pelican editions, lining a low shelf. I hear a Miles Davis record, *Porgy and Bess*, playing in the background. The place is Gainesville, and I am six, and, looking up, I see the back door of our house. The kitchen is empty; curtains fall across black windowpanes. It is night, the shouting has stopped, and the door is open: someone has left.

Thirty-five years later, I asked my mother to fill in a few gaps. In calling forth her memories of her life with him, or of her life alone with two small children, I risked her anger at me—at *me*—as if I were my father, and she were delivering the last word on our marriage.

Instead, she told me about the music and art he'd introduced her to, and about the poetry they'd read, and about the wild parties they'd thrown for their friends at the University of Florida, Butler and Charlie and Conrad and Maud and others whose faces still appear from time to time in my thoughts. As my mother spoke about her young marriage, the muscles around her mouth loosened, and her eyes grew soft. Her gaze, which rested directly on me, seemed to become clear—her memories felt good to her—and, exhaling smoke from her cigarette, she smiled.

Three years later, after she'd told me that I looked like my father, I stood in her Black Mountain living room, her sick bay, and, peering down at my feet and bare legs, at my shirt coming untucked from my shorts, said, "I guess you're right, Mom. I do look like Dad."

"That's all right, Don," I remember her saying. And I answered, "I hope so, because there's not a lot I can do about it."

But what about the will? Looking back it can seem to me

that the existence or nonexistence of my grandfather's will is important less as a substantive question in its own right, more as a quandary, unanswerable, mysterious. In remaining mysterious, the will became—and becomes—a source of power, the power, in this case, to enact betrayal and deprivation. My mother had betrayed the memory of her father. Was she now, in her abandonment of her children, giving *us* permission to betray *her*? Was she inviting us, one last time, to fight and be punished? Who would disappoint whom, and who could suffer with the most grace? And who, in the war between a mother and her children, a war of shame, could ever set things right?

A few days before my sister and I left Black Mountain, I sat on a stool at the empty hotel bar, and, as I'd done before, opened the yellow pages to Attorneys. This time I saw, as if it had been listed only that afternoon, a name that struck me. Maybe my grandfather had mentioned it once. I picked up the phone and dialed the number, and a receptionist answered and connected me to the lawyer, who, when asked if he'd known my grandfather, Don Self, acknowledged that he had. Had they worked together? Yes, he told me, they'd worked together. In order to preserve client confidentiality he could not speak about the particulars of their business. However, in an approximate way, the lawyer ratified my suspicions: My grandfather had wanted a trust for his daughter and grandchildren to be provided through his will. But then he'd died.

What to do? It was not a matter that could be safely discussed with my mother. I remember watching her sit up in bed. First, she had to reach out with a hand and clear the plastic air hose from the mattress, so as not to crush it beneath her. Next, working from an inclined, sideways position, she lowered her legs off the bed—leverage—and, using her full strength, shoved herself upright. She hunched forward and supported herself with weak arms, her hands placed beside her knees on the edge of the bed's high mattress, her feet, blue from her poor circulation, hanging down like a child's. She was still coughing, of course. I remember that she would look around the room with a fogged, faintly wary expression on her face, as if she did not quite understand where she was, or whether the locals were friendly. Merlin, her black cat, whom she believed to be a direct reincarnation of the Arthurian necromancer, would sometimes be curled beside her, and she might speak to him in the cooing voice she used when conversing with cats, even those she didn't know. I remember that the house smelled like ash, though my mother had stopped smoking. Everything—rugs, curtains, bedspreads, tasseled chair cushions, Merlin—remained smoke-permeated. It drove my sister crazy. I remember holding Terry in my arms when, one afternoon, standing outside in the scratchy, untended yard behind the house, she broke down because our mother had become argumentative over the nurses who'd come that day for interviews. Terry and I piled in the car and escaped west toward Asheville, then up the Blue Ridge Parkway in the direction of Mount Mitchell, which I'd climbed on my bicycle when I was in my twenties. Now, crossing from slope to slope, rounding the parkway's elegantly graded bends in the road, I could occasionally see, looking from the car's rolled-down windows, tiny squares and rectangles in silver and white and black and red—barn and farmhouse roofs dotting the valleys below. As we ascended, the air temperature dropped, and we passed through clouds that had settled in the mountaintop hollows. I leaned back in the passenger seat, watching for hawks in the sky, and my sister told me about her family's boat trips on Puget Sound, about her children's schools, and about her painting—still lifes and landscapes, mainly. Listening to her talk about her life, I was reminded of car rides across the mountains with my grandfather.

I do not, however, remember what day it was—the end of Terry's and my stay in North Carolina was close—or the hour (a memory of sunlight falling through my mother's living-room windowpanes, illuminating dust in the air and a section of far wall, makes a picture of afternoon becoming evening), when, after opening her eyes and finding me near, my mom whispered:

"Don, I know we need to talk about things."

That is what I remember her saying. Maybe she said something slightly different. But it was clear what she was referring to. Everything was clear. I nodded my head.

She called, "Merlin, come here, Merlin."

"Merlin!" I said.

The cat leapt from the floor to the bed. "There you are. How's my Merlin?" said my mother.

I scratched his back, and he lowered his chin and raised his tail, and his fur shedded away in tufts.

The day before Terry and I left North Carolina, we drove into Asheville and shopped for fresh fruit and vegetables. The grocery store had decent fish, and I bought sole. My sister and I had finally set in place the health-care and legal provisions required for our mother's care. We'd scored a victory of sorts. Our mother had suggested a willingness to consider radiation. It looked as if the oil spilled beneath her house would be cleaned up after all. Terry and I loaded the car with supplies, and, on our way home to Black Mountain, we listened to a radio show playing field recordings of Appalachian music—old, plaintive ballads describing betrayal, repentance, redemption, loss in love, alcoholism, and conversations with the devil. These days, it is not merely the subject matter, familiar and disturbing, that makes this music of Tennessee and the Carolinas difficult for me to bear. Rather, it is something heard in the singing, that discernibly nasal, heavily accented, prayerful quality of voice—the voice of the region in which my mother and her family had been born—that can cause me to reach out and shut the music off. That day with my sister, I listened with something like joy. I cannot speak for Terry, but I believe that she, too, heard, rising up from the hissing, popping shellac, the cadences and the rhythms and the slightly downward-falling inflections that occur, in milder form, in our own voices.

We got back to the house and unloaded the groceries into the kitchen. It was a gorgeous, bright day on its way to ending. As on previous days, I was wearing my version of my father's clothes. Our mother was dressed and moving about. I offered to cook. Dinner was simple. There was the fish, simmered in a pan on top of the stove. There was asparagus. Rice. A salad. Glasses filled with iced tea. While I made dinner, my mother and my sister sat at the old, dinged-up wooden table that had been, during the years when Terry and I were growing up, our family's dining-room table. This table had been bought by my father and the woman for whom, back when Terry and I were five and six years old, he had left my mother. Now it was here.

And in my mother's living room, stored in a plastic urn inside a cardboard box, our grandmother's ashes rested on a shelf.

What I am trying to say is that, in a way, we were pretty much all present, in one form or another, in my mother's house that night—all of us except our mother's father.

But then he got invited, too. My mother invited him. I remember this with clarity, because it was astonishing to hear, astonishing, as well, to wonder, as I have over the years since, about the truth regarding her father's will, though I realize that I will probably never know the truth, and must only imagine my mother in the days immediately following her own mother's death, my mother sick and with the incipient awareness, surely, of the severity of her illness. I see her collecting my grandmother's ashes from the undertaker, bringing the ashes home and placing them on the shelf, maybe only then pulling the old paperwork from a box or a file, and making her way up the hill to the lawyer's office in town. I wonder, imagining such scenes, what had led me so deliberately to pursue, in my thoughts and in my actions, the idea of my mother as a thief, when, just as likely, she was no thief, merely a woman who was sick and alone and scared and grieving, hoping for a better life, one that was not ever going to come, not in this world.

That evening at the dinner table, my mother said, "I remember. I remember. There was another lawyer. Granddaddy said that there was a lawyer in Asheville."

I recall that the sun was setting. The light outside the partly curtained window above the kitchen sink, the window facing west, with a view of trees, had been growing dark. I turned and looked at my mother. Maybe I was holding a spatula or the pan of cooking fish.

She went on, "What was his name? What was it?" Then she pronounced the name. It was the name of the man with whom

I'd spoken a day or two before, whose phone number I'd got out of the phone book, the man my grandfather had contacted about a trust.

She said, "Kids, I'm going to make things right. I'm going to make things right."

At that point dinner was ready. I plated up, and we gathered around the table, just the three of us—or the six of us, or however many of us were, in body or in spirit, present in that room—and, as I recall, someone said about the fish, "This is good," and I said a silent prayer that my mother would get well and not die, not ever die, and the next day my sister and I got in the rental car and fastened our seat belts and headed up the hill toward the highway. We drove east across the mountains. Near Lake Lure, we stopped at a roadside stand, where I bought sourwood honey in a mason jar that I tossed into my suitcase. We continued out of the mountains, up and down the foothills, and through rolling farmland toward Charlotte. At the airport, Terry and I dropped off the car and boarded a courtesy bus that took us to the terminal. I checked my suitcase, and, when the time came, she and I walked off down the long concourses leading to our different gates. My sister went one way and I went another.

That night when I got to my apartment I discovered that the honey jar had been smashed to pieces during the flight. Honey and shattered glass were everywhere.

PART VI

A t the time when I began trying to draw my father into literary conversations, we were living in a Miami tract development that featured homes whose exteriors evoked a variety of architectural schools. Most were Modernist; several looked like Modernist churches. Ours had a pale green, Bauhaus-style façade, and was settled into an unpruned hammock of overhanging trees and dense, humid-looking flora that appeared as if it might one day advance across the narrow yard and engulf the house. It didn't matter that the driveway ended in a busy road, or that neighbors were close. A jungle enclosed us. You couldn't see in, and you couldn't see out.

The house itself was a single-story rectangle with bedrooms taking up the eastern half, a thin strip of kitchen in the middle, and, looking toward the end opposite the bedrooms, a dining area and a small sunken living room. Sliding glass doors opened from the dining and living rooms onto a screened-in patio and pool out back. My sister and I spent a lot of time splashing in the water, then running into the air-conditioned house for something cold to drink. It was my job, once a week or so, to skim debris off the pool's surface, vacuum the bottom, and, using a little plastic test kit, check the chlorine. Caring for the pool was dispiriting. The patio, like the property's front and sides, was surrounded by hardwoods and tall pines, whose branches, arcing overhead, shed decomposing leaves, brown needles, and powdering bark that filtered through the screen and made a scum on the water. The trees blocked much of the day's light, leaving the pool shaded during the long subtropical afternoons. These factors may have contributed to the algal buildup around the tiles marking the waterline. Algae showed on the bottom, too, and in faintly discoloring streaks that curled down the deep end's walls. I periodically went at the algae with brushes and chemicals picked up at the pool-supply store by my father on his way home from teaching. We moved into that house in 1972. During the year of our residency there, the algae crept out of the pool and claimed sections of patio, darkly filling the veins and cracks that gave texture to the concrete. I remember dragging aside porch chairs and our glass-topped table, pouring acid over the contaminated spots, then hosing everything down. Sometimes on weekend mornings I got up early and swam a mile's worth of laps—one of many things I did in solitude—while my parents and sister slept. On afternoons after school, I could often be found lying facedown in the water, staring through a face mask at the light show of refracting shadows cast across the surface by passing clouds and windblown treetops. In anticipation of one day getting scuba certification, I'd begun collecting gear, a piece at a time. I had a tank and a secondhand regulator, and every now and then I'd buckle these on, fasten a weight belt around my waist, plunge into the pool, and sink to the bottom, where, six feet under, I'd sit, breathing.

Out on dry land, I was coming into consciousness of the books on display on my father's shelves in the living room. In imitation of him, I'd begun collecting and exhibiting my own paperback collection, works by Jules Verne, H. G. Wells, Robert Heinlein, Arthur Conan Doyle, J.R.R. Tolkien, Charles Dickens, Lewis Carroll, and Edgar Allan Poe, along with leftovers from earlier eras of childhood, books about boys' adventures in crime solving, soldiers' daring escapades during wartime, and heroic athletes' triumphs on the playing field. Surely my father had his own era's versions of books like these lying around his bedroom, back in the days in Sarasota, when he'd first encountered my mother.

Some years before she died, my mother confided to me that during the years of their courtship, both when she and my father were in high school, and after they'd gone to college—he in North Carolina, she in Florida—my grandmother Eliza, my father's mother, a daughter of old Virginia, had counseled him against his choice, softly discouraging him on the grounds that my mother's people were from Tennessee, and therefore not ideal. Quiet disapproval had been in the air, my mother told me, even after she and my father had married. It is easy for me to imagine that my mother felt unsure of her welcome in the Antrim family, not because I knew my grandmother to be a snob, though she may have been, but because my mother so often felt maligned in the world. What I mean to say is that her fears about her mother-in-law's prejudices may or may not have been credible. Either way, they point to her anxiety over her desirability.

His, I suppose, was never much in question. Not too long ago, I began sorting through a collection of color transparencies, Ektachrome slides he took during the sixties and seventies. They're pictures of our family for the most part, though a number show places we visited, interiors and exteriors of houses where we once lived, old acquaintances of my parents whose faces I recall but whom I cannot name, and cats and kittens we had as pets. I don't own a projector or a movie screen, so, in order to get a good look at the pictures, I've been using a handheld viewer. Pushing a slide into the little black box turns on a hidden light that illuminates the image, which is magnified through the lens. Each slide is stamped with the month and year when it was developed. The slide's white cardboard frames have faded since MAY 70 and APRIL 71 and JAN 73; they're brown at the edges now, and beginning to look antique. It occurs to me that the process of loading and looking at them is, like the slides themselves, of another era: it's entirely manual. Several times I've had the feeling, while holding a transparency in sunlight to check, before fitting it into the viewer, for shades and tints that show if it's upside down or right-side up (a winter sky's blue, a meadow in green, the sandy white of a Florida coastline)—I've had the feeling, dropping the correctly aligned slide into the aperture, easing it down to make the light go on, and staring into the black box, that I am not merely looking at pictures from another time; I am peering into the lost past.

It's something about looking into a box. Children's stories are rich with imagined devices that serve as passageways to other worlds. A passageway might be as simple as a mirror or a narrow door at the back of a wardrobe. It could be an abandoned well down which a character falls or, more famously, Alice's rabbit hole. All that is asked of us, when reading about children who tumble down rabbit holes, is that we not judge too harshly the quality of their encounters with talking rabbits.

Otherwise we'll miss out on an adventure. Both rabbits and children are our guides, and we must follow where they take us. The images on my father's slides, looked at through the lens of the battery-lit looking glass, might lie opposite a window on a faraway land. This impression is an ocular effect. The exterior perimeter of each slide is delineated by the dark interior perimeter of the box, making it appear as if only a small area (the image) within a larger realm (the unseen world beyond) is actually apparent to us. This effect can be resolved into a question. If we were able to perceive a bit more through the viewer, might this vaster realm, the world of which the slide is one small piece, also come into existence? Do other worlds radiate out into the room in which we sit staring into a box?

If only we could *see*. Inside the box, images float. Blackness lies around them. Landscapes, houses, animals, people—they all look as if they are meant to appear for a time, then vanish. Which is exactly what they do, the moment the slide is inserted and the light in the box goes on, the moment the slide is removed and the light shuts off. We've received a glimpse of something, or of someone: a visitation. Reds—there are in my father's collection several pictures featuring roses—stand in a curiously forward position in relation to the viewer; they hover above their backgrounds in a way that evokes old 3-D images. People seem full-blooded and alive, yet their features are often hazy. The light around them glows.

A few slides show my uncle Eldridge, my father's brother, reclining in the stern of a sailboat—my father, for a few years in the 1970s, had an affinity for sailing—drinking a beer on Biscayne Bay. Eldridge's drinking has not yet overtaken him; he's in his mid-thirties here, and looks fit and healthy. As always, he wears a beard—it's tinted red from the sun and is trimmed close to his face, shaped by the razor in the manner in which I, when I wear a beard, trim and shape mine—and, also, as always, he sports a gold chain. He's tanned and happy. In just a few years, though, he will begin in earnest his retreat from the world. He will disappear from our lives and exist increasingly in solitude, leaving his small Sarasota apartment only to drive across the Siesta Key bridge to his nighttime job as a prep cook at a restaurant on the Gulf of Mexico. Throughout the eighties, as his alcoholism intensifies, and as his weight drops and he becomes sicker, unable to eat, his solitude will turn to isolation, and, eventually, he will die.

But all that takes place later—it's what's to come. In the meantime, in the pictures shot by my father, Eldridge looks comfortable and content, stretched out in the back of a boat, beside a dark-haired woman wearing a head scarf, plastic sunglasses, and a yellow bikini. She has her hand in a bag of potato chips. I do not recognize her. Is she my uncle's companion? Does she call him Eldridge or, as his friends did, Bob? In the distance behind her we see choppy water beneath a bright subtropical sky. This is the sky that I remember from that time, from that place. It is full of dampness and gray-green heat. Storms emerge from it. It appears to be lit from within.

Or has my memory been altered by an effect of the box? Remember that inside the viewer, things really are illuminated from within. That gray-tinted sky appears again and again. It's there above the pines and in mottled reflections on the pool behind the Bauhaus-style house, and it is there in a picture of my father himself, standing before a palm tree whose green and brown fronds, spreading out to fill the frame behind him, suggest a hugely oversized headdress. Here is my father adorned as tropical potentate, youthful king of some island tribe that will one day disband and scatter to the four corners. He wears sideburns and, as he did through most of my childhood, a mustache. His hair is black. Turned away from the camera, he glares down and back over his shoulder at a photographer who might be crouched beside him—or kneeling, paparazzi-style, on one knee?—in order to capture a pose that will have the appearance of, well, a pose. In this picture, it is difficult to know who is "subject" to whom. My father looks into the camera lens, into the eye of the photographer, and, subsequently, back out of the lens of the black box, out of the light and into the eye, as they say, of the beholder. His expression is guarded, narrow-eyed, furtive; he looks, I think, as if he wants to see but not be seen, or as if, like Alice's white rabbit, he is in a hurry to get somewhere. But where? The light in the box flickers on, and, just like that, he lets us see that there is something we can't see. Then he's gone. We have been warned of his departure—it's in his eyes—yet it is unclear whether we are invited to chase after him. Who snapped this picture? Was it my mother? Did she kneel at his feet, peer up through the camera lens, and, seduced, ready to follow him, say, "Stop a minute. Stand in front of that palm tree. Come closer. Turn toward the camera. Now hold still"?

And what is it, exactly, that my father lets us see and not see? What is it that he *knows*?

A literature professor, he made his living thinking and talking about books. I was a teenager in Florida when I began asking him about the titles on our shelves at home. "What about this?" I would say, holding up a collection of Theodore

149

Roethke's poems or an English novel. Or I'd take down a volume on linguistics—at fifteen I developed a minor fascination with the nontechnical opening chapter of Thomas Pyles's *Origins and Development of the English Language*—and say, "Dad?" I remember that he might nod his head and utter a noncommittal word before turning away, as if my curiosity embarrassed him; and I wonder, now, looking back, whether to accept his reticence as part of a Virginia tradition of masculine taciturnity—I think of my father's father and uncle and those roadside plaster birdbaths—though this likelihood leaves open the question of what my father, standing in our living room thirty years ago, might have been trying without words to tell me about books and their place in his life. Did I somehow know, did I *feel*, growing up in houses stocked with stories and poems and the correspondences of dead writers—and watching him go to a job that mandated enthusiasm (however guarded) for literature and its study—that books, whose contents could not easily be shared between us, might become the foundation of an intellectual inheritance that could be mine to take pride in, or ignore, or deride, or, years after I'd left home, and when that home was no more, stubbornly invent?

I bided my time. What can I accurately remember, today, about a boy who, in a long-ago time and faraway place, sat on the bottom of a swimming pool, breathing through a tank? What was in his mind?

When I was born, my father was an army lieutenant stationed at Fort Knox. Later he would transfer to Fort Bragg, in North Carolina, where he would have command of a tank battalion, and where my sister would be born. My mother told me that my father was not with her in Sarasota when she had me. She was alone, she said, except for her parents. Because I was crying, she told me, her mother came into the room and, I don't know, snatched me up and carried me away from her, from my mother. She'd not been able to hold me when I'd been a newborn baby, because her own mother had wrested us apart. "We didn't get to bond," my mother told me when I was an adult, and added that she thought that my father, had he been present at my birth, might have intervened and stopped her mother from stealing me from her arms. But my father was in Kentucky. Because of his absence, my mother and I were unable to forge the attachment that a mother must make with her child in order for each not to wander through life longing for the other. That was what she believed, and told me, when I was about thirty years old.

It strikes me now that my mother, in telling that story, was exercising her failing power to ordain my future. In telling me what I couldn't possibly remember, she hoped to tell me a truth about myself. She wanted me to see matters as she saw them, and stay close to her. There's nothing unusual in this, I suppose. Our parents' lives before we are born take place in a kind of mythic realm, a realm of the imagination, and our mothers' and fathers' power to shape and interpret our lives, to tell us who we are, even in our adulthood, requires our under-standing that, because they inhabited mythic time, and because their existence has brought about our own, they remain for us immortal and all-seeing, just as they were when we were too young to survive without them. In telling me a story about a rift between us at my birth, my mother tells me that I will al-ways search for her, because to me she will never die.

My search through other women began with a girl who

took off her clothes and, her hand reaching up to hold mine, lay down on the floor beside my bed. She was eleven and had curly hair. I was twelve. My family was living in Virginia, in the main house on a farm called Fiddler's Green, thirty minutes west of Charlottesville, where my father was a professor. The girl, G., had come for a sleepover party with me and my sister and my friend Peter. Peter was my junior high school classmate, and G. was the daughter of a colleague of my father's, a man who, the year before we moved to Fiddler's Green, had come in the middle of the night to our house on Lewis Mountain Road, in Charlottesville, carrying a loaded gun at his side. Anyway, that night at Fiddler's Green, sometime after my parents had shut off the lights and the house had gone quiet, G. snuck through the door that led between Terry's bedroom and mine. Peter was asleep in my room's other bed. Earlier, G. had been forward during our kids' game of strip poker, deliberately losing hands. Then it had been bedtime. When she came through the door, she got right under the covers with me, and we began kissing with our mouths closed. She was naked. She held her legs together. Her breasts had just begun to develop. I remember her on top of me. We hugged and kissed and tumbled around quietly. My erection was painful. I kept it hidden inside my pajamas. I recall the bright moonlight that came through the white curtains my mother had put up in my room. There were three windows. Two looked out over Fiddler's Green's small formal boxwood and rose gardens. Those roses that I mentioned earlier, the ones which, in pictures looked at through the slide viewer's lens, seemed to detach from their branches and rise up to meet the eye, grew in the garden beneath my bedroom. In bed that

152

night with G., I could see, in the moonlight, my desk and chair, and some toy racing cars and a strip of track on the floor, and my bongo drums, and the side of the bookshelf separating the two twin beds. I could see Peter, his shape, curled beneath a blanket on the other side of the shelf. It might have been Peter's movements in bed that caused G. to slide down from the mattress to the floor, where she would not be seen by him if he woke. I gave her one of my pillows, and she reached up to hold my hand. How long did we manage to keep ourselves awake? It seems to me that we held hands even after we'd fallen asleep. By morning, she'd snuck back through the passageway leading to my sister's room.

The next day, after she and Peter had been picked up and taken home by their parents, I got in the car and went somewhere with my mother. I remember our drive over rolling hills, on roads bordered by white fences. We drove toward, then alongside, the Blue Ridge Mountains. It was summertime, and the car windows were rolled down. Wind stormed around the interior of the car, and, every now and then, smoke and ashes from my mother's cigarette scattered and flew into my eyes and nose. I began to feel nauseated from cigarette smoke and summer heat and the rising and falling of the car as it passed over the pastured hills.

Or did I feel sick from my adventure with G.? An anxiety came over me, sitting in the car with my mother. I had done something to divide us, and nothing would ever be the same again. We drove through the Virginia countryside, and I leaned partway out the passenger-side window and let the wind blow against my face.

I don't know what happened to G. after that. She may have

children of her own now. It wasn't long before my family moved away to Florida, first to a house in a large subdivision on what was then the western edge of Miami, then farther south, to the Bauhaus-style house. Eventually I would return to Virginia for boarding school. I recall hearing, around the time that I graduated from Woodberry Forest, or shortly after I'd left home once again, for college in New England, that my old friend Peter had driven his car off the road and crashed into a tree and died. The accident happened, I believe, at night. I don't know whether he'd been drinking.

But there is another story I want to get to, one that involves books. It takes place in Florida, in the Bauhaus-style house, the house surrounded by palms and tall pines. It was there that I began reading self-consciously, systematically, and acquisitively, which is to say that I began to take notice of myself in the act of reading, possibly because connections *between* books were becoming apparent and meaningful to me. J.R.R. Tolkien's *The Lord of the Rings* trilogy was enjoying its hippie-era popularity; you had to read it, and I did, in elegant volumes that came packaged as a boxed set. That led to other boxed sets. Many were available in 1972, released by publishers hoping, presumably, to profit from readers' hunger for experiences that could replicate, or nearly replicate, the Tolkien trip, which was perceived by many people as a vast world-reordering—an end to unjust war and postindustrial tyranny—carried out by barefoot commune dwellers. It wasn't Tolkien's argument that sold me on *The Lord of the Rings*, however. I was attracted, I think, to what might be called the narrative's spirit, which is expressed technically in the rules and laws that both create and govern Middle Earth's complex network of societies, each with its own language and history, its codes of behavior and its embattled relationship to good or evil, even its own magic. The awakening in adolescence to systems of social and psychological interdependence, magical and otherwise, was, for me, a quiet revelation. I wanted more multivolume flights into inner space. Books let me in on my own capacity for following connections—the peaceful farmers may live far from the shadows beneath the mountain of death, but they can reach that darkness if they listen to the talking trees; a reader may doubt the legitimacy of worlds not his own, but he can traverse those worlds nonetheless, if he keeps turning pages—and, before long, the connections that mattered were to other books.

One was H. G. Wells's *The Island of Dr. Moreau*, the story of a mad scientist who uses a remote island as a kind of fortified preserve for his living creations, half human and half animal, the mutilated products of laboratory experiments in the nineteenth-century pseudoscience of vivisection who roam the jungle in states of agony and rage at their master. *The Island of Dr. Moreau* spoke to me. It came in a set of Wells's science-fiction novels, *The Invisible Man*, *The War of the Worlds*, *The Time Machine*, *The Food of the Gods*, and so on, each, as far as I was concerned, a fairly thorough rendering in metaphor of some aspect of the human condition. I had C. S. Lewis's *Out of the Silent Planet*, *Perelandra*, and *That Hideous Strength*, which, as it turns out, are about alternate worlds only to the extent that they are, like the epics of Tolkien, also about Christianity; and I remember, too, a set of truly strange works by E. R. Eddison, a mostly forgotten English writer of sometimes impenetrable medieval-style romances. Eddison's *The Worm Ouroboros*—the title refers to a dragon swallowing its own tail, graphically illustrating circularity and never-endingness—prepared me for *The Nibelungenlied*, the "Song of the Nibelung," a reading assignment set for me in the tenth grade by my German teacher as punishment for disrupting class and shirking on homework. Frau Webb thought she was going to stump me, but I was, by then, very conversant with the smiting of heads and quaffing of mead, the aura of celebrated death that can be found in northern European sagas.

I remember a girl named Eileen who sat behind me in German class. I used to turn around in my desk frequently, to look at her legs. School in Miami in the 1970s was an erotic ordeal, because the girls came dressed for the beach. Sometimes when the bell rang I was forced by my erection to stay at my desk for a minute or two before staggering off to the next period. I carried my books in front of my dick.

Anyway, the books. It wasn't only their interiority that mattered to me. I cared for their materiality. A book of good weight, that opened nicely to reveal clean text on grained paper, functioned satisfyingly as the physical container of its familiar or unfamiliar worlds, making more concrete, more apparently real, the author's inventions. Many years after the time which concerns me here, after I was grown up, living in New York and publishing books of my own, I visited the Folger Library in Washington, where, in a subterranean vault, I was shown the library's immense collection of early printed works, including the world's largest accumulation of first-folio and quarto editions of Shakespeare. For some reason, my guide had no problem with my handling the books, and I walked along the shelves, taking down not only Shakespeare but

Chaucer and Sir Philip Sidney. I remember opening Sidney's *Arcadia*, a massive and dense prose work, a sort of cosmology of Elizabethan love and politics, written for the author's sister, the Countess of Pembroke. The pages of the volume in my hand showed, in almost stunning relief around each letter, the heavy impressions left by the press. The array of letters shaped into words, words into sentences, and sentences into paragraphs seemed perfect, as if the book's maker had precisely known the textual disposition most likely to encourage the eye's movement down the page. Published near the close of the sixteenth century, the *Arcadia* opens with a dedication to the Countess:

> *Here now have you (most deare, and most worthy to be most deare Lady) this idle work of mine: which I fear (like the Spiders webbe) will be thought fitter to be swept away, then worn to any other purpose. For my part, in very trueth (as the cruell fathers among the Greekes, were woont to doo to the babes they would not foster) I could well find in my harte, to cast out in some desert of forgetfulness this child, which I am loath to father. But you desired me to doo it, and your desire, to my hart is an absolute commandment. Now, it is done onelie for you, onely to you: if you keepe it to your selfe, or to such friendes, who will weigh errors in the ballaunce of good will, I hope, for the fathers sake, it will be pardoned, perchance made much of, though in it selfe it have deformities. . . .*

I was hooked by the words on the page and by the page itself, pliable and tough, stained, deep in the paper's weave, with flecks of dark color. The binding was limber. I was breathing quickly. I'd been curious to see the Folger's books, yet had not anticipated their durability and powerful tactile appeal. They'd existed for such a long time. As my guide and I rode the elevator back up to the main reading room, I wondered who I might call on the phone. To whom could I blurt out the excitement of peering into these books? As I remember, I called my father, who listened patiently while I described the sensation of holding the *Arcadia* and the *Shepherd's Calendar* and *A Midsummer Night's Dream*. What I am getting at is the idea that books do not in all cases merely *convey* the content on their pages; in some fundamental respect, books, especially the most beautiful, shelter and accommodate their contents.

I wanted beautiful books. I wanted to know what my father knew but would not, or could not, standing uncomfortably before the shelves in our sunken living room in Miami, say to me. And so I began to make a library of my own.

One night, a month before Christmas, 1972, we were sitting at dinner in the house in the jungle, when my father made a proposal. His proposal was not directed toward me in particular, yet it contained an acknowledgment of, if not an answer to, the questions I'd been asking him about literature. He offered a Christmas in which he, my mother, my sister, and I would give and receive books. We'd keep things simple and not overspend. We'd have a book Christmas.

I remember thinking: *Books?* Wait a minute! What about all the other stuff? But I understood that I was being invited to put myself forward as a serious person. If books become one's way of looking at and piecing together society and the world, then exchanging books might be an initiation into authentic membership in the world.

It was quickly decided. My sister was enthusiastic and so was I. I even knew what books I desired. I'd seen, in a store in South Miami, an imposing two-volume annotated edition—elegantly boxed, naturally; that was all-important—of Arthur Conan Doyle's Sherlock Holmes stories. They became the gift to go after, and for several weeks I dropped hints and made a point of declaring my passion for hardcovers.

Christmas was a time in my family when hopes for happiness got ritualized and, as it were, acted out. The holiday required protection from the discord which ruled our typical existence, and the quieter-than-usual days leading up to it came gradually to seem an end to my parents' difficulties and the advent of a peaceful era in our lives; and, to that end, actual gifts, particularly my father's for my mother, had a lot riding on them. My father's proposal of a book Christmas might have been his attempt to lessen the psychic weight attached to the things placed beneath the tree, though when I think about my mother's part in such a Christmas, I wonder whether the burden was much reduced. She had many talents, my mother, and, in spite of everything, she had her pleasures, but reading wasn't at the top of the list. Occasionally I'd see her with something by a writer she and my father knew socially, a university acquaintance with a career as a novelist or poet. However, apart from keeping up with the output of friends from southern academia—and I'm not sure whether she did so more than halfheartedly—she wasn't what you'd call a reader. She didn't voice curiosity about whatever might be found in books, and she did not ask questions or make observations relating to books in the world. I never heard her, when I was a teenager, express feelings brought on by something she'd read.

How lonely for him, I thought from time to time when I was growing up. Then I'd wonder: Why did they get married? And a moment later I'd wonder: Why'd they get married *twice*? The days when I began exploring myself through reading were also the days when I started analyzing the problems in my home, and I suppose I took my mother's indifference to books as disdain for the communion, through print, between an author and a reader, that inner experience we take from written words. Did she feel contempt for my father, who nurtured this experience in his students?

It's not a bad question. I didn't want that boxed Sherlock Holmes set for nothing. The powerful detective is a master of the universe. His deductions release us from the anguish of living in an inexplicable world. I couldn't unravel the logic of my parents' marriage, but, reading Arthur Conan Doyle, I could briefly master my feelings of helplessness. Mastery was the aim in acquiring books in sets. Sets promised the triumph of completion. It wasn't sufficient to read a story or two; I wanted totality. The box housed its separate volumes as interdependent parts of an intact world. To conquer the realm of the boxed set was to acquire strong magic—my father's magic. I could not have known, at that time, that I was stealing from my father, but I was. I was beginning to study and prepare for writing. I don't recall what I gave my parents or my sister for Christmas in 1972. I do remember that I got the Holmes stories, though in paperback rather than in the edition I'd fantasized about.

The night before Christmas, my parents fought. My father had violated the provisions of his own proposal, and arranged around the tree a number of elaborately wrapped packages, clearly not books, for my mother. Of course my sister and I didn't expect him to give her only books. Just the same, seen against our expectation, the abundance was notable.

It was a long and dark night. My mother got falling-down drunk. She had a practice during her bad spells of stopping at the door to my room. She would teeter in the doorway and bellow at me that I was not participating properly in the life of our family, and that she didn't care about whatever I might or might not *want* to do—I could act any way I wanted when I got to be eighteen, because then I'd be paying rent around here, but until then I didn't have rights—and I could just go to hell. Or she might isolate a shortcoming, like my poor performance in school, and attack me for it in a manner that suggested I was the root cause of our family's misery. Invariably I would be divided in my feelings: I was furious with her, yet worried over whether she might fall. It was a sorry predicament. At some point on Christmas Eve she engaged me. I don't remember what she said, or whether I ran out into the middle of her fight with my father, out and down the little steps into the living room, where the tree stood with its lights on. I remember my sister pleading with them to stop. At about three or four in the morning, there was a crash. Our mother had fallen into the Christmas tree and brought it down on top of herself. I remember her crying out as if she might die. My sister and I ran into the living room, where our father was struggling to raise her. Our cats were hiding beneath chairs. The floor was littered with glass shards and broken ornaments. Water from the tree stand had splashed across everyone's presents. My mother was claiming to have broken her arm. But she hadn't. We got her off the floor and, somehow, into bed, and then, I don't remember, my father swept up the mess and righted the tree, and a while later the sun came up.

I slept, some. I woke to the sounds made by my sister fixing our parents a special Christmas breakfast. I got up, and Terry was in the kitchen cutting fruit. I doubt we said much to each other.

It was a long time before our parents came out for Christmas morning. My mother needed coffee and time in bed. She may have bruised herself in her fall, but she did not—I suppose because of the occasion—tell us if she was in pain. It was a forgotten incident. She lay against pillows and picked at her breakfast until around eleven o'clock, then hauled herself to a chair near the tree. It took her a while to arrange her coffee cup, cigarettes, lighter, and ashtray on a table near the chair. Once she was settled, we started opening presents. Everyone was quiet. My sister had done everything she could to save Christmas.

We took turns with our gifts. I opened the paperback Sherlock Holmes set, and, later, a few other books, and then some non-book things. Clothing, probably. I remember my father inspecting something from my mother and forcing a grateful, affectionate smile—she'd found just the right thing—a smile meant for us as well as her, and for himself, because he, too, wanted to salvage the morning, along with, I guess, his dignity. Mainly I remember my mother as a captive of the gifts he lavished on her. At the time, she had begun a minor collection of Art Nouveau objets d'art—candlesticks, bud vases, copper bowls, serving trays overlaid with silver—and my father, as I remember, gave her a number of such pieces that year. Again and again, my mother was compelled to put down her cigarette, tear open a package, and smile and plastically exclaim at him. It was hard to watch. She had no control over her alcoholism. She didn't understand this. And neither did we.

PART VII

O ne night when I was ten, in the year before we left town and moved to the farm at the bottom of the mountains, a man carrying a gun knocked on the front door of our house on Lewis Mountain Road, in Charlottesville. My father answered—he'd been waiting for this visit—and the armed man, a literature professor, my father's friend and colleague at the university, said hello. My father and mother had until that moment been fighting. It was a bad fight. My father thanked the man for coming and invited him in. The gun, as I remember, was a long-barreled revolver holstered on a coiled western-style gun belt that the man held in one hand. The gun hung at his side, down near his knees. He walked into the house, carrying the gun, and my father closed the door. I watched from above, from the dark landing at the top of the hallway stairs, and could see, looking down between the banister's white railings, my father and his friend as they crossed the entryway into the living room, where the man said, "Hello, Lou."

"Hello," my mother said to him. He placed the gun belt on the coffee table beside her chair. Did my father mix our guest a cocktail? I had not yet learned to measure, over the course of a night, the predictive correlation, in my parents' lives, between drinks and fights, though I'd become accustomed, during the years when my mother and father had been divorced—when she, my sister, and I lived in our one-story brick house on Eighth Street, in Tallahassee, Florida—to seeing my mother with her bourbon on the rocks.

We'd been a family of an incomplete sort, the three of us in that house, the house across the street from the church with its rusting steeple detached and laid on the ground. In my memory, the churchyard grass was patchy and weedy—not brazenly wild in the manner of a yard surrounding a derelict house, but unkempt. Was the church lacking funds for its own upkeep? Was that why the steeple lay abandoned on the ground?

On the other hand, I can remember that the churchyard was, in fact, tidy and well tended. The borders of the walkway leading from the street to the church doors were, it seems to me now—*can* seem to me now—neatly trimmed. Maybe weeds and tall grass grew only around the perimeter of the steeple itself, inside the narrow zone that could not safely or easily be reached by lawnmowers and edging tools. On Sunday mornings, a nicely dressed congregation gathered on the church's mowed front lawn, and later, during the service, their singing could be heard coming from inside the building. It is possible that the weeds in my memory grew not in the pretty churchyard but on the vacant square of land adjacent to it, the roughed-up, improvised neighborhood playground on the other side of the recumbent steeple.

Then again, wasn't the church itself as badly in need of paint as its amputated top? What sort of people went to that church, anyway? I was eight years old, then nine, and I climbed on their steeple, ran its length, jumped from it, and tumbled in the weedy, or, possibly, lush grass. The steeple was like the peeling hull of a boat that had years before been dragged inland and stripped of its teak and brass. Nowadays, I expect that I might find it there in the churchyard, were I to visit our old house in Tallahassee. Of course, this is unlikely. Almost forty years have passed since we left that town. I have not returned, and neither has my sister. In the late 1970s, our mother went back as a student, commuting from Miami in order to complete the work required for her doctorate. I do not remember her ever speaking about the house or the church or the steeple. And so, unlike other places where we lived either with or without our father, places which, for one reason or another, I have revisited—Sarasota, Miami, Charlottesville—that place, with its giant trees hung with Spanish moss, its smells of pine, its sand roads near the center of town, and its nearby lakes and slow-moving black rivers, exists for me with the power of a fantasy.

In this fantasy, a man not my father comes to visit my mother and take her to dinner and a movie. When he arrives for their date, two Chihuahuas leap from the passenger side of his car, tear across the yard, and chase our cat. Who is this man? Why is he here? What about our father in Virginia, to whom I write postcards saying, "Dear Dad, I am fine. How are you?" and which receive replies that read as pleas: Can't I tell him something about my life? Won't I tell my father what I am doing?

What *am* I doing? I am lying awake at night, sped up on amphetamines, fighting to breathe. I am playing the Beatles' "Day Tripper" on pretend drums, with my friend John Covington faking guitar. I am trying to get the courage to leap from the high diving board at the Florida State University pool, and I am riding my red bicycle. I practice gymnastics with the Tallahassee Tumbling Tots, though I fail to progress past a cartwheel. I like a blond girl named Susan in my third-grade class, but she moves away. For years I will dream of finding her. Alone in my room, I build model ships and airplanes, impatiently spreading paint across the hulls, guns and fuselages *after* the models have been built, because I can't wait to see them finished. I want my chair, my desk, the walls of my room painted orange, but it never happens. A fireman, his wife, and their son live in the house next door to us, and the son's band, The Other Side, practices in their garage, and I go over and sit on a speaker. The room smells like burning electrical wiring. One after another, the band's brothers and friends disappear into Vietnam. I am a Cub Scout. Our black-haired den mother lets us scouts hurl water balloons off the roof of her house at pedestrians walking by on the far side of a tall hedge. She has a son we never see, though we hear him playing a horn in an upstairs room. Down in the yard, we goof off and tackle each other, messing up our blue uniforms. One day, the Cub Scout powers-that-be fire our den mother, and soon I am standing in a treeless, suburban backyard learning slipknots, or sitting at a kitchen table painting candy canes onto a coffee cup for my mother. I know in my heart that something is wrong. I want my father to come back to us for good, instead of once each month. I am a No-Neck Monster in *Cat on a Hot Tin Roof* at the university theater. A sign on a bathroom door backstage forbids flushing the toilet during showtime, yet I manage to flush in spite of this, and the sound fills the theater. The following year, when I play Young Macduff, my picture is in the paper, accompanying a notice about the production. In the caption I am "little Donnie Antrim." The photographer has asked me to scream, but I am too self-conscious to scream for the camera, yet try to fake mortal agony anyway, and so it appears in the newspaper that a freckled boy is laughing the laugh of the insane while a dagger is sunk into his back. Many years later, in New York, I will meet the man who played Macbeth. He is appearing as the monster in a downtown production of *Frankenstein*. He tells me that Lady Macduff is alive and well and living in Massachusetts.

Back in the fantasy, however, my sister and I are riding in the car with our parents. Our father has driven down from Virginia for one of my parents' hostile weekends, and we have been visiting grandparents in Sarasota. Before returning to Tallahassee, we stop in Clearwater. At an aunt's house, Terry and I get a surprise. The aunt, who can't keep a secret, asks us how we feel about our parents' decision to remarry. Are we excited? Are we happy? This is wondrous news to us, and we jump up and down and run around our aunt's kitchen table and tug on our parents' clothes and shout up at their faces, "Are you? Are you getting married? *Are* you?"

It is not long before we are in the black Beetle again, driving westward into the land of truck stops, alligator-filled lakes, and horse farms. In Gainesville, we park in front of the Episcopal church that we attended before our parents ended their marriage. After our parents and the pastor meet privately in his office, we enact a brief rehearsal. Then we do the real thing. We walk as a family down the aisle of the empty church. My sister carries a bouquet, and I, wearing short pants, bear the rings. It is my job to hand over the gold band that my father will put on my mother's hand.

I remember my anxiety, that day in the chapel. I was waiting for my cue. I knew that my parents' rings were in my pocket, but was afraid nonetheless that I would fail in my mission. Would I reach into my pants pocket and find that I had lost the rings? Would I drop one on the floor? And might it roll away beneath a pew and disappear?

But wait. Were the rings in my pocket, or were they sitting on a pillow, a velvet pillow that I carried like a serving tray? Or were they in a box—a box in my pocket? Or was one ring in one pocket and one in another? Whose ring was in which pocket? I have a memory of a voice—my father's?—saying to me, "Be careful not to lose those." Where in the church could I have lost my parents' rings, though, that they would not be found?

We packed up the little house in Tallahassee. A moving van carried away our things. Before leaving for Virginia, I walked across the street and, standing in the grass beside the church steeple, wept over the friends I would never see again. We put Zelda Fitzgerald, our cat, in a cage in the backseat of the car, then climbed in ourselves and drove across the state line into southern Georgia and on from there through the successive landscapes that marked the stages of the journey north. We went through the Georgia pine stands, around broad, man-made lakes, and across red hills. We continued through the Carolinas, through fields planted with corn and tobacco, past neglected, rotting barns whose painted roofs advertised pecans and fireworks. Whenever my sister or I saw, looking out the car windows into the distant west, a big range of hills, we imagined that we had come to the Blue Ridge Mountains. The Blue Ridge belonged to our father's world.

In Charlottesville, we unloaded into a house on Lewis Mountain Road, down the way from Memorial Gym and the university tennis courts. The house was not big. It was painted white, with a front door that I want to remember as red but which was probably also white. We had a narrow yard that sloped uphill in back; there was room to throw a ball, but not enough space to play a game. In the basement were broken walls partitioning unlit places that smelled as if they might open onto passageways running beneath the streets and houses, down into the earth. Above the basement, the kitchen was off-white and cozy, smaller than the kitchen at Fiddler's Green, where we would move the following year. Every time we relocated—and we did so every year or two, as if life were a steeplechase through rented houses—we would go into the new rooms and paint the walls and uncrate the books and dust off the flower vases and sort the silverware and hang the pictures and roll out the rugs in a matter of days, as if in a hurry to produce a home that might be an improvement on the one that had come before, and in which we could forget or at least put in the past the unhappiness that had come before, knowing that once the chairs were arranged in the new living room and the beds in the new bedrooms had been made, it would come again.

A number of years before she died, my mother told me that soon after her second marriage to my father, she realized that the woman with whom he'd had his affair was still a presence. She told me that after we moved from Tallahassee to Char-

173

lottesville, she, my mother, had sometimes been greeted, during social gatherings at the homes of my father's Virginia colleagues and friends, with questioning looks, as if the people she met were uncertain about whether she was really his wife.

Her rival was a poet who lived in a distant state. Several times, after I'd finished college and moved to New York, I came across a poem or group of poems by her. Standing in a magazine shop or a bookstore, I searched the lines for images, for a voice, that might connect me, however tenuously, to my parents in their youth. One day, I discovered a letter she'd written to my father. The letter was from a time when I was little. It was pressed between the pages of a paperback copy of Tom Stoppard's *Rosencrantz and Guildenstern Are Dead*. I'd stolen the book from my father's shelves before leaving home for boarding school, and I'd subsequently carried it to college and, from there, to New York. How had I never before seen this letter? Had I not read the play? I found the letter in the book in the 1980s, when I was living on the Upper East Side. I remember that I refused myself permission to open the envelope and look inside. The letter hadn't been written to me; it didn't belong to me; it wasn't meant for me. Reading it would be unethical, maybe even immoral. Weeks went by—or months, it seems to me now—while I maintained a furtive attachment to its forbidden, unknown contents, which I absurdly hoped might offer me a bit of insight into my family's history. I regarded the writer, who had played such a significant part in our troubles, as a kind of outcast relative. Could a piece of her lost mail help me understand what had happened to my mother and father?

I read the letter. I remember that it was nighttime. I was sitting on the sofa in my tiny apartment's tiny living room. I opened *Rosencrantz and Guildenstern Are Dead*, took out the envelope, extracted and unfolded the pages inside, and began. I recall a passage describing a new green dress that the writer had worn to a party. Both dress and party were described in teasing, playful, overtly erotic language, language that makes clear her desire for my father's adoration and jealousy. I felt guilty and embarrassed. Maybe I had expected the letter to contain literary chat of a sort that I imagine my father wishing he could share with my mother, a reference to, say, French poetry or new directions in criticism. I folded the love letter, stowed it back between the pages of the book, and replaced the book with the other novels and plays stacked in crooked piles underneath the platform sleeping loft in my bedroom. Twenty years and a half-dozen apartments later, I don't know where *Rosencrantz and Guildenstern* has got to.

Most all of my mother's stories—the angry tales she told me, before and after she got sober—about her life with my father contained, I think, a notion of self-improvement as a process of gathering insights into other people: if we name the faults of those who have hurt us, we will be shielded from pain; if we can collect evidence to justify our anger, we will overcome shame; if we pity our betrayers, we will not have been betrayed, mishandled, misunderstood, or left abandoned. But what happens when the ordeal of abandonment is—as I think it was for my mother, and for me with her—life itself?

Near the very end, in the years immediately before she was diagnosed with cancer, and even after she'd begun radiation, my mother dreamed that she and I would go on a trip together, a journey of sorts, the two of us in a car, touring the countryside, stopping at inns. She proposed this many times. "Would that be nice, Don?" she might ask, after naming a region—the Florida Keys or some wild stretch of the Pacific Northwest—in which we might travel around, talk about art, and get to know each other better.

"That might be nice," I would say to her. My mother wanted to go on a honeymoon with me.

"Will you think about it?"

"Sure."

"We could go in the fall."

"*This* fall?"

"Is that too soon?"

"I don't know. Can we talk about it when the time is closer? It's hard to see that far ahead."

"Oh. Well, I know you have a lot to think about."

"I guess I do." Unhappily, I would imagine checking into a rural bed-and-breakfast or a surf-side cabana with my dying mother, who would humiliate me. She'd talk loudly at the dinner table, and treat the waiter poorly. I could picture myself glancing to the left and the right, wanting to hide or, failing that, apologize to everyone we met.

Whenever I imagine such a trip, I am inclined to remember one that we did take, in 1982 or 1983, when she was struggling to get sober. We'd met at her parents' house in Black Mountain. At the end of our stay, I loaded her suitcase and mine into her station wagon, and we started the drive to Florida, where I would spend a few more days before returning to New York. We drove south through the mountains. Halfway home, in St. Augustine, we stopped for dinner. I remember that we parked the car in front of a white house, a Florida bungalow built, probably, in the 1930s or '40s. It featured louvered windows, a stone porch with a painted ceiling, and a flowering tree in the yard.

The sun was in the west. Sea smells were in the air. "Look at that pretty house, Don. I've always liked it here so much. I'd love to live in a house like that," I remember her saying.

We stood and looked at the house. Then we walked down the street to a local restaurant, a fish house. After dinner, we walked past the little house again, got in the car, and drove south. The ocean was to the left. The sun had almost set. We passed a few hotels, then a long stretch of deserted beach. I stopped the car, got out, and walked across the sand. I left my mother in the car by the roadside. The surf was high, as I remember. I took off my shirt, rolled up my pants, and waded in. After my swim I dried off as well as I could, got back in the driver's seat, and drove through the night.

But where was I? North Carolina? Georgia? Florida? New York? Or back in the house on Lewis Mountain Road in Charlottesville? Or the farmhouse we rented in 1968, after we left Lewis Mountain Road?

The farm's grounds were surrounded by fields full of cows, and the front yard rolled downhill to a rocky creek. Out back, at the top of a hill, was a white barn filled with hay bales. If you walked up the drive past the barn, then down the other side of the hill, you came to a pond. On the pond's far bank, beneath overhanging branches, stood the remains of a mill. The pond was brackish and not good for swimming. One afternoon, I watched a gang of boys from a family squatting in the ruins of an old house across the road march in a line up our driveway. There were five or six of them. They carried fishing poles made of sticks. I followed the line of boys, stopping to watch them from behind a fence at the top of the hill near the barn. They were gathered on the pond's small, rotting dock. In a short time, they hauled in three or four dozen perch. A boy would bait his hook with kernels of canned yellow corn, drop his line, and immediately bring up a fish, which he would lower, flopping on the hook, to the planks of the dock. Another boy, an older brother, would stomp on the fish's head. The dock was stained with blood, and the sun was setting behind the mountains, and I was twelve years old, and it occurred to me that God was feeding these children, but that He didn't have to feed me, because my family could buy food. We had clothes, books, and a fire in the fireplace. Every night during the cold months I collected wood for our fire from the woodpile behind the garage.

One autumn night when my father was away on a trip, I went out back for logs and boards, and found a dying bird. I called to my mother, who came out and stood in her nightgown in the cold. The bird's wings were broken, and its eyes looked terrified. Should I kill it? We owned a rifle, and I proposed to my mother that I might shoot the dying bird. I'd already shot and killed, on another chilly day, a snake that I'd found crossing the front yard. There'd been no reason to kill this snake, but I'd done it anyway, using a BB gun. I'd told myself that the snake was dangerous, and I'd chased it around trees and boxwood bushes and the elevated stepping-stone left from the days when Fiddler's Green's inhabitants kept horses. Later that night, the minister of the Episcopal church in Greenwood, a family friend, stopped by for a visit, and, when he got out of his car, I ran to him, crying, "Look! Look!" and he lowered his head and peered down at the snake's body coiled inside a paper bag, and, as he looked, my pride turned to shame.

Should I now destroy the injured bird? Here was a chance to redeem myself, to kill humanely, in the spirit in which a farmer might, not pointlessly but with compassion. It was an opportunity to be a man in my mother's eyes. She gave me permission to get the rifle from the upstairs closet. I made sure the rifle was loaded, then walked back down the stairs, through the kitchen, past the giant old Southern Coop freezer on the back porch, and out to the yard, where I shot the bird, I guess. I don't remember shooting it. Maybe I waited in the dark for the bird to pass away on its own. Or maybe I never got the gun at all. Maybe my mother and I found a cardboard box and, using a folded towel as a cushion, made a bed for the bird, a bed like those we made for our cats to lie on when they gave birth to litters. Did my mother and I carry the bird inside the house full of cats and kittens? Or maybe the bird was gone when I returned to where it had lain on the ground. Had it hobbled away to die? I remember my mother's face. She looked at me as if she understood that I was trying to understand something. She was willing to see me kill the bird. But did I? And if I did, was she standing beside me when I pulled the trigger?

In 1970, my father left the University of Virginia for a job in Miami. We packed up the farm and headed back to Florida. I was twelve, going on thirteen, and Terry was eleven, going on twelve, and the shift from old Virginia to new Miami was, for the two of us, even at our ages, especially at our ages, unsettling. What was this flat, hot, paved-over place, this place made, as it looked to me upon first arriving in the early 1970s, entirely of one-story houses, crowded freeways, and shopping centers?

In Miami, all our houses were different and the same. Two came with swimming pools. One was noisy from a nearby road, and another was surrounded by trees and bushes—that was the Bauhaus-style house—and another had a cathedral ceiling. These latter two were next door to each other, their properties joined by a path leading through the brambles and vines. When the lease on the Bauhaus-style house was up, we sorted the pots and the pans, rolled the rugs and folded the linens, boxed my mother's fabrics and her sewing machines, my father's library. Like four refugees ducking beneath branches and stepping over roots, we carried the lot, one armload per trip, from the old place to the new.

But what about the man with the gun? He sat down in the living room in Charlottesville, placed the gun, in its holster, on the coffee table around which he and my parents were gathered, and, in a steady voice, began to speak. He was a good-looking man, I remember, a popular teacher and something of a power in the English department. His voice was deep. He had come to calm my mother and father. The gun, I should say, was there to calm them. The man did not know, and my parents did not know, that I was watching from the dark landing at the top of the stairs.

My sister watched with me. Didn't she? We crouched together on the landing. And did she follow me down the stairs, across the front hallway, and through the open doorway to the living room? I remember hearing the man tell my parents that they could annihilate each other; though, if this was their choice, one or the other of them might as well pick up the gun—there it was in plain view on the table, next to their drinks—and complete their work of fighting to the death. I came down the stairs in my blue pajamas and stood among the adults. I can still hear, in my memory of that night, her voice, and I hear my father's; I hear them speaking together: "Don, go back to bed. It's past your bedtime. Everything's all right. Run to bed, Don. Off you go."

Did I get a kiss goodnight? I retreated to my room and lay awake, trembling. Would she kill him? Would he kill her? If the killing took place after the man with the gun had gone home, how would it be done? With a knife taken from a drawer? Where would the killing take place? In the kitchen? In their bedroom? Would there be blood? Would there be screaming, then silence? And would silence feel like relief? Would she go to jail for murder? Would he go to jail for murder? Could I be called to testify in a court of law? How would I testify? Who would be guilty? Who would be innocent? Would my sister and I tell the same story? What story would we tell? Would I tell the truth? What might the truth look like? Would I know the difference between right and wrong? Would someone come and take my mother away? Would someone take my father away? Would my sister and I become orphans? Would we be alone forever after?

In 1981, the year I left college and moved to New York, twelve years after my father's Virginia colleague had come to our house with a gun, my mother was taken to Mercy Hospital in South Miami. She was admitted, my father told me, for alcoholic hepatitis. She was held at Mercy for a few days, not many, until she was considered sufficiently detoxified, hydrated, rested, and nourished, and, after that, she was discharged, and a short time later my father had to drive her to the hospital again, and the process was repeated, and, a while after that, she went back again. Then, quite abruptly—or not at all abruptly, considering the long progress of decades—my parents' marriage was over for good.

Over the next two years, my mother would be forced to attempt sobriety or die. These were the years when her father, then in his seventies, and I, in my early twenties, created our adult friendship. It was one of those friendships that are sometimes available between the nonconsecutive generations in broken, unhappy families.

I was a teenager when my grandfather retired from his job as a junior high school principal in Sarasota. He and my grandmother sold their large, Spanish-style house on Wisteria Street and moved into a cramped and unattractive condominium, which they hated. After that, circumstances allowed them to become regular visitors to the western Smoky Mountains around Asheville, just east of that part of the world from which they had originally come, and, in 1977, the summer I graduated from boarding school in Virginia, they retired from their retirement and bought a derelict bungalow on Third Street in Black Mountain, intending to restore it and, eventually, move in. Would I like to join them, to spend my summer before college working on an old house? Yes, I would be happy to come to North Carolina and work on the house.

And yet, once in Black Mountain, I had a tendency to abandon my grandparents to their painstaking and methodical, stooped-over, Presbyterian labors; each day, I fled the house in order to drive aimlessly over mountain roads that passed by indigent farms and even more indigent churches. I had no concept of work. What was wrong with me? When would my life begin? Looking back on that time, I have an impression of myself performing a kind of fitful, mild-mannered revolt against— what? Anhedonia? Boredom? My family? Or it was a protest against southern Protestantism in general, which I associated with prohibitions and taboos in a variety of forms, expressed negatively in the self-destructive or work-obsessed temperaments of, it seemed to me then, everyone I knew. But protests against the denial of pleasure bring no pleasure. In the spirit of someone with nowhere else to go, I turned the car around and returned to the house on Third Street, picked up steel wool or a rag, and found something to scrub.

The day came when we got around to the windows. These were painted shut and badly warped. There was no question of replacing them; they would be removed, their panes razored clean, the frames stripped with fine sandpaper, or, if too profoundly rotten, disassembled and rebuilt. This was heartbreakingly deliberate work. I remember windows pulled out, holes in the house. Inside the casements lay dust and dirt, dead animals' tiny skeletons, the windows' rusted pulley wheels and ancient counterweights, canvas sacks stuffed with lead shot and tied off, their ropes broken. I remember my grandfather's old man's hands worrying the wood, delicately touching, like a blind man reading, the surfaces of things; it was slow work that he seemed determined to make slower, as if work of any sort were equivalent to an act of obstinacy. My grandmother's style was all harshness and haste—she attacked her chores. And I remained lazy and sarcastic; the screen door was always slamming behind me. Nonetheless I was attracted by my grandfather's patience, by the care he took with this broken house. It wasn't that I suddenly understood the value in a job well done. Far from it. It was that for a moment—a romantic moment destined to resonate and grow in magnitude over the years—I hoped (and this may have been a fantasy that I wanted to have about the man) that my grandfather had something to pass on to me, to teach me. And I imagined (because it did not occur to me to ask him) that what he had to teach me concerned the beauty in labor that is invisible to others, work that seems superfluous but isn't, and that no one except the worker will see or even necessarily appreciate. The windows, when they went back in, slid up and down at a touch.

Fifteen years later, when my grandfather was nearing ninety, in the days right before he began having his heart attacks, and long after he and I had been brought together by my mother's hospitalizations, we took drives together along the roads that led over the mountains, rambling, all-day excursions that infuriated my grandmother, who feared for his health. We'd stop on the shoulder in a hollow or a narrow valley, and my grandfather would get out of the car, unzip his trousers, and urinate; a frequent need for this was caused by his heart medication. Always, he drove. Bourbon, I suspected, was stashed in the tire well in the trunk—his guilty, exciting secret. At some point along the way, generally when we were far from home, out past Hendersonville, he might say, "Have I shown you the new stretch of the Blue Ridge Parkway that goes around Grandfather Mountain without touching the mountainside?" or, "You've never seen the Carl Sandburg house, have you, Don?"

"No, I haven't," I'd say, and he'd turn the car around, and off we'd go to our new destination.

Today, I cannot recall those outings without thinking back to the early 1980s, when he and I took turns caring for my mother. I do not know, can't say, how many hospitalizations she endured—four? five?—on her way to sobriety, or how frequently she quit drinking for a week or a month, attended a series of AA meetings held in smoke-filled rooms, and then went out and picked up a glass. During these years, my grandfather and I became adept at hearing, in her voice on the telephone, the specific sounds—a softly rising inflection, like a plea uttered by a child, ending a whispered sentence; or a barely audible sigh—that told us she might be feeling defeated and hopeless.

"Your grandmother and I think we ought to drive down to Miami and spend some time with your mother," he might say to me during one of our conversations.

Or, if my grandparents had recently done service, I might say to him, "Mom's coming out of the hospital at the end of the month. Why don't I fly down and pick her up and take her home?"

Or my grandfather might say, "Don, your mother is going to come to North Carolina for a week. She needs a rest."

If my mother were on her way to Black Mountain, I might head south myself, and the four of us, three generations, would come together for a brief spell as a family.

Would it be wrong to remember those as happy times? Is it

perverse to imagine, to believe, that she, in her struggle to live, in her nearly dying, took care of us?

Of all the stories from that era in my mother's life—the era in which I found myself perpetually on call, waiting for bad or good news from Florida or from North Carolina—one stands out. This is the story of the time she came closest to drinking herself to death.

In the spring of 1983, she finished a monthlong detoxification at South Miami Hospital, in Coral Gables. The patients on the ward were diverse. One was an emaciated man with a long beard. He'd spent his life in the Everglades drinking whiskey. Another, a Cuban man with an enormous belly who'd worked as a baggage handler at the airport, had, each day on the job, while loading and unloading suitcases from conveyer belts and motorized carts, drunk two to three cases of beer. I remember my mother telling me that he had a wife and baby. There was a young blond guy who'd made and lost a fortune as a cocaine dealer; until entering the hospital, he'd carried thousands of dollars in his pockets. And I remember an aeronautical engineer who'd retired to the Florida Keys. According to my mother, he later piloted a plane of his own design into the Gulf of Mexico.

But that's not the story I mean to tell. The story I'm thinking of begins on a Saturday night in New York. I was with friends at the Madison Pub, a bar on the Upper East Side. It was early, still light out. We'd ordered a round of drinks—I was nursing a Manhattan, of all things—and it crossed my mind to call my mother and see how she was getting on. There was a pay phone at the rear of the bar. I excused myself, went back, and dialed her number. It was a collect call. Her phone rang a dozen times before the operator broke in and suggested that I try later. I rejoined my friends but could not enjoy myself. Eventually I went home to my apartment, where I called her again. The phone rang and rang. I'm not sure why I did not assume—it would have been logical—that she was out for the evening. Why did I let the phone ring? I was right, though. She picked up.

I waited for her voice.

"Mom? Are you there? Mom?"

After a long moment, she made a crying noise. The receiver clattered—did she drop it?—and the line disconnected. It was a few minutes past eight o'clock. I called my grandfather in Black Mountain and explained to him that I had to go to Miami.

"Tonight," I said.

At that time in my life I could not have considered any possibility but going to her, yet could not have afforded plane fare without his help. He promised that he would have a ticket waiting at La Guardia airport. I phoned my mother again, and her answering machine picked up. After the beep, I cried, "I'm coming, Mom!" I threw some shirts in a suitcase, locked the apartment behind me, and ran down the stairs, out of the building, and into the street, where I collided with a taxi. I bounced off its side as it rolled to a stop, and a rear tire almost ran over my foot. I jumped into the back and asked to be taken to the airport as fast as possible. The driver turned and asked, "Hey, are you all right?" and I panted, "I'm fine, I'm fine." I rolled down the window and took deep breaths of air. At the airport, I ran to the counter of the airline my grandfather always used. The ticket was waiting. At the gate, the flight was boarding. We took off shortly after ten, and, sometime around one o'clock, the plane landed in Miami. I waited for my suitcase to appear on the baggage carousel, then went to the taxi stand, got a taxi, and gave the driver my mother's address. As I remember things now, she was living in an apartment that I had never before visited. But is this right? Surely, on earlier trips, I had stayed with her in the very place that I was now speeding toward. Have my memories converged to make some new, universal memory? The taxi headed south, then west. After thirty minutes, we stopped at a newly built duplex townhouse, one in a series of identical two-story buildings on a numbered street in a nondescript neighborhood. I paid the driver, grabbed my luggage, and started up the walkway. The lights were on in my mother's house, and the front door was hanging open. Strange. Had she heard my voice when, earlier in the night, I called to her through her phone answering machine? Had she left the door open for me? Near the entryway stood a couple of empty wine bottles. They looked as if they'd been set out for the milkman. Bottles lay on their sides on the living-room floor. More stood on the kitchen counters. I stood in the brightly lit living room, calling, "Mom? Mom?" It was two in the morning and the house smelled awful. The kitty litter had not been changed, and my mother's white cat, Flora, had shat on the carpet. "Mom?" I called, and heard movement overhead, a footstep.

She was at the top of the stairs.

I saw her feet. Then I saw the hem of her nightgown. She came down one step at a time. Little by little, she appeared. She held the bannister. She lowered herself halfway down the stairs and, with both feet on one step, and with her hands gripping the railing, turned to peer out over the living room.

She looked to the left and the right, and up and down, slowly. "Mom, it's me," I said, but she did not seem to hear. "Mom?"

"Who?" she whispered.

As my mother aged, and particularly during the period when she was sick with cancer, I would grow accustomed to seeing her frightened, or helpless, or frail; she could look, at times, like a stranger to me. That night, I had the feeling that she was, even as she stood on the stairs, dying. What did she see, looking at me? She did not see me. I don't remember how many times I said, "It's me, Mom," before she turned and, tugging with her arms against the bannister, went back up the stairs. It was as if my arrival had been part of her dreams, or as if she'd heard a noise, come down to investigate, and found nothing. After a moment, I heard her walking overhead. I followed her up the steps.

She was lying in bed, shivering. I pulled the sheet and bedspread over her. Beginning with her hands, one, then the other, I re-created, from memory, the massage she'd given me when I was a boy in Tallahassee and I'd had my asthma attacks. She had come into my room and whispered, "Easy, honey. You're going to be all right. I'm here." She would massage my back, my arms, and my hands, pressing her thumbs into my palms, then kneading her way up my arms to my shoulders. She pounded my shoulder blades and my back, in order to loosen the congestion blocking my lungs. Before she finished, she would retrace her movements and hold my hands in hers once more. I remember feeling that she was squeezing the fear right out of me, pushing my distress down my arms and out my fingertips; and I remember that my panic would subside when she held me, and, as the asthma pills took effect, and even as my breathing remained difficult, I could close my eyes and sleep.

That night in Miami, her hands were clenched—I had to pry them open—and she was sweating. Her skin, her unwashed nightgown, the damp sheets on the bed, the room itself, smelled of alcohol and nicotine. I rubbed her neck and shoulders, and lightly pressed the heels of my hands against her back. Later in the night she became aware of who I was, and, in a few quiet words, let me know that she'd been hallucinating. Dragons and other monsters flew at her from the corners of her bedroom. I remember looking around, trying to picture her visions. What would it be like to watch black serpents crawl from behind a chair or a dresser? I sat beside her on the bed and whispered to her that I wouldn't let the monsters hurt her.

Sometime after four, she slept. I got up, turned off the light, and closed the bedroom door. No, I must have left the door open a tiny bit, just in case. I went downstairs and cleaned the dishes she'd left in the sink and on the counters. I changed the cat litter and put new food and fresh water in the bowls on the kitchen floor. I gathered bottles and threw them in the trash. There were over twenty. She'd had them delivered.

I stayed a week. She remained in bed for much of it. I went to a store and bought food. She sat against the pillows, and I fed her soup, soft-boiled eggs, and canned peas and corn. She refused a trip to the hospital or the doctor. Instead, when she was able, near the end of my trip, after she'd recovered enough strength, she got in her car and took herself back to Alcoholics Anonymous.

During the two decades since then, I have often thought of my mother in terms of diseases and symptoms. Ever since she'd been a girl in Tennessee, her life had been marked by illness. Illness defined her relationship with her own mother, whom she outlived by only a year, and, sadly, illness defined her relationship with me. That she was, throughout my childhood, sick, the nightly victim of a terrifying Jekyll-and-Hyde transmutation, I learned to take for granted, even as her grandest symptoms, having become in the eyes of her family more or less expectable, even normative, seemed almost to vanish inside the stormy routines of her, and our, everyday life.

In recent years I have noted how surviving children can find themselves reappraising their mothers and fathers, who might appear braver, stronger, and more beneficent in death than in life; and maybe it is true that, as time goes on, and we, their children, survive and lament their passing, we nonetheless continue in the hope that we will one day truly know our parents, as they will know us.

Near her life's close, I lost the fortitude, the ability, the heart to be with my mother. For a time, I referred to her, in thought and in conversation with others, not as my mother but as Louanne. Her parents had sometimes called her by this name, but my father and my parents' circle of friends always knew her simply as Lou. In thinking of her as Louanne, I pretended to an objectivity of perspective that I did not, nor will ever, possess, and, in doing so, I pretended to myself that the coming loss of her would not hurt, and that in the absence of suffering I would go forward, a free man.

A week after I flew by night to watch her descend, in delirium tremens, the staircase in her Miami duplex, I went into her study, where she kept sewing supplies, files holding papers that she'd accumulated during her years of teaching, and her typewriter. In an hour, she would drive me to the airport, and I would return to New York. I sat at the typewriter and wrote her a note. It was brief. I told her that I loved her, and that others loved her, and that we who loved her wanted her to live. I hoped she'd make it. I left the note scrolled in the typewriter. Many years later, she told me that she'd put it in a safe place and kept it. She never drank again.

Five years have passed since her death. I'm not sure whether I can say, now, what her Christian name means to me. She was my mother. Her ashes have yet to be scattered. They remain, to this day, in a box in a closet at my sister's house. Maybe before long Terry will fly with them to Charlotte, North Carolina, where, at the airport, I'll meet her. We'll join up at the car-rental desk, get a car, put our mother's ashes in the backseat and our suitcases in the trunk, and head to Bridges, in Shelby, for barbecue, then continue west toward the Smoky Mountains. We'll drive past Chimney Rock, around Lake Lure, up past Old Fort, and down into Black Mountain, where we'll stay a night or two at the Monte Vista, the hotel that was our base when our mother was dying. I'd like to sit on the Monte Vista's porch one more time and gaze out at the mountains known locally as the Seven Sisters, before getting up and continuing on highways bordered with kudzu and corn, gas stations and pecan emporia, horse farms and flood canals, office parks and ocean resorts, straight through South Carolina,

Georgia, and Florida, all the way to the Keys, to Islamorada, where, on the Atlantic side of the island, there is a beachfront lodge that my mother loved. I hope to go there, take the ashes out of the car, and, with my sister beside me, walk to the water with them.

ACKNOWLEDGMENTS

For their support and encouragement during the writing of this book, the author thanks Jonathan Franzen, Nicholas Dawidoff, Allan Gurganus, Jeffrey Eugenides, David Means, Melora Wolff, Matthew Klam, Christine Hiebert, M. E. Bowles, Janice Deaner, Pamela Leo, Amy Azzarito, Melanie Jackson, and Jane Shapiro. Thanks to Andrew Wylie, Tracy Bohan, Elena Schneider, Katherine Marino, and Amelia Lester of the Wylie Agency; and to Jonathan Galassi, Lorin Stein, Kevin Doughten, Lisa Silverman, and Annie Wedekind of Farrar, Straus and Giroux. My thanks to Deborah Treisman, David Remnick, Bill Buford, Dorothy Wickenden, Field Maloney, and Rhonda Sherman. I thank the National Endowment for the Arts, the John Simon Guggenheim Memorial Foundation, the Corporation of Yaddo, the MacDowell Colony, and the Dorothy and Lewis B. Cullman Center for Scholars and Writers at the New York Public Library. Last, I am grateful to my family for their tolerance and understanding, and I am thankful for the generous and loving support of Fran Dilustro.